RAISING CHILDREN WHO MAKE RIGHT CHOICES

Diane Tohline

Scripture quotations were taken from the *The Amplified Bible* unless otherwise stated. *The Amplified Old Testament* copyright © 1965, 1987 by Zondervan Corporation, Grand Rapids, Michigan. *New Testament* copyright © 1958, 1987 by The Lockman Foundation, La Habra, California. Used by permission.

Scripture quotations marked MSG are taken from *The Message*, copyright © by Eugene H. Peterson, 1993, 1994, 1995, 1996. Used by permission of NavPress Publishing Group.

Raising Children Who Make Right Choices
ISBN: 978-1-4675-3687-5
Copyright © 2012 by
Diane Tohline
www.DianeTohline.com

Cover Design: Gabby Vonigas
gabbyvonigas@gmail.com
Text Design: Lisa Simpson
www.simpsonproductions.net

Printed By BT Johnson Publishing
www.BTJohnsonPublishing.com
Toll Ffree: 1-866-260-9563

Printed in the United States of America. All rights reserved under International Copyright Law. Contents and/or cover may not be reproduced in whole or in part without the express written consent of the Publisher.

Dedication

To Stephanie, Jordan, and Lauren…

Without you in my life this book would never have been written. You have given Dad and me so much joy. Together we have made memories that will last our lifetimes, and the journey continues. Each one of you truly is a gift from God with special and unique personalities that have made our lives exciting. I have learned so much in the process of raising you. It has been a joy!

For all the children who deserve a home where they can be trained to make right choices early so their lives can be bright and fulfilling…this book is for you!

Acknowledgements

Jayce, Barbara, Debby, Jan, Marva and Verna—thank you all for believing in me and encouraging me to write down what was in my heart concerning *Raising Children Who Make Right Choices*. You saw in me what I could not imagine possible. For your love and friendship I will be eternally grateful.

Jayce, my precious husband, thank you for your faith-filled support and for partnering with me in raising our children.

To Jordan, my son and editor…thank you for the countless hours you spent in helping me get this on paper.

Table of Contents

The Story of This Book 9
Parenting is a Journey
    The Preparation 13
    The Destination 17
    The Journey 21

The Purpose
    We Are Created by His Purpose and for
        His Purpose 27
    God's View Point 33
    Like Arrows in the Hand of a Warrior 33
    Difference 41

Our Role as a Parent
    You are Important and Extremely Significant 49
    Job Description: Mom 57
    How Can We Do This Job? 63
    A Vision 69
    Gatekeeper 73
    Trainer 79

Laying the Foundation Upon Which to Build
    Build for the Future…by Making a
        Strong Foundation 87
    Following a Blueprint 91
    Three-Part Beings 101
    Equipping our Children with Knowledge 107
    Training Our Children 115
    Choices 119
    The Value of Words 127
    Listening and Obeying 133
    Training Their Ears to Hear 139

Boundaries and Discipline
    Discipline 151
    What Godly Discipline is Not 155
    Discipline Keys 161
    Respect 171
    Boundaries: Setting Guidelines for Your Family 175
    Disrespect and Challenging Authority 181
    How to Correct 205

Putting it all together
    Putting it all together 217

The Story of This Book

Since I was in my 20s, I have carried a passion for families and children. No matter what I did, the wellbeing of families grabbed my interest. It wasn't long before I started wondering where this passion came from…and it wasn't long after that before the answer to this question came as well: God *put* this passion inside me!

For years, I have done my best to help parents—teaching classes, preaching at churches and women's conferences, and coaching mothers one-on-one. Wherever an opportunity has arisen, I have taken hold, doing the best I can with the gifts God has given me.

Eventually, people started telling me, "You need to write a book." Um…

I am a speaker, I used to think, *I'm not a writer!* I have grown to feel comfortable speaking in front of people; words flow easily from my mouth—from my heart! Writing is different, though… when I thought about writing a book, it felt more threatening. *Sure*, I thought, *I'll write a book. Maybe. Eventually.*

But time passed, and this seed continued to grow. I'll admit, I tried to suppress it at times! I tried to *not* water the seed—but there it was, steadily pushing up through the ground. I even made excuses: "God, there are lots of parenting books out there. Parents don't need *another* one!" But the more I argued with God, the more He showed me where my insights—where my "book"—fit into *His* BIG PICTURE view. He showed me the insights I had that could help parents raise children who *make right choices*.

When I got laid off my job, I started the process. The first step of the process was believing that God was truly telling me to write this book. (I thank Him that He is so patient!) It has been a long journey—a journey that required me to realize I had something to say that was different from what has been said already.

This book will take you on a journey. It is more than a "how to" book; rather, this book unfolds a story—God's story, from His BIG PICTURE view.

God has a plan that will work for *your* family. And the most important part of this plan is you, the parent!

As parents, we often tend to put our children first—because of the intense desire we have for their wellbeing and success. But *you* are who matters! You matter to God, and *you matter to your family*.

As you begin this journey, I encourage you to take each chapter and let it build the foundation for the next. By the time you reach the end, you will have a strong, long-lasting foundation in place, and you will have the blueprint in hand to build the structure of your family!

A note to dads: If you are reading this book—I am glad. I know I have spoken a lot from a mother's perspective—perhaps because I am a mother and I speak primarily to women. However, that does not negate the powerful impact you, as the father, will have with this understanding! Thank you for joining in—I am excited that you are here.

PARENTING IS A JOURNEY

The Preparation

Being a great parent is not
something that 'just happens'
It requires preparation!

Little girls grow up playing house. Throughout elementary school, they keep a cradle beside their bed packed with two or three 'sleeping' dolls. By middle school, girls have determined their babies features and picked out their names.—"I'm going to have *three* girls and *two* boys; the oldest girl will have dark hair and green eyes; then the boys will be twins, and I'll name them Jack and Jason and they have curly blonde hair and brown eyes.; and then I'll have two more girls with blonde straight hair"—and by the time these girls are in high school, they not only know what their wedding will look like, they also know exactly what their bridesmaids will wear and how their faceless husband will style his hair for the big day.

Little girls grow up *dreaming*.

When I married my husband, the first part of my dream came true. When I found out I was pregnant, my dream was fulfilled!

But babies are not the end of the journey; the dream continues. Babies become toddlers, and toddlers become children. Children become young adults, and young adults grow up.

Each of us wants to be a good mother, and we want to raise great kids. We want to unlock the potential our children possess so their future can be wonderful! We want to raise well-adjusted children who are prepared to launch into their lives. And of course, we want to do all of this with love, with joy, and (God help us!) with peace, too.

Parenting can be hard. It is ever-shifting and ever-changing. It is so unpredictable! Just when we figure it all out, it changes again. Whether you are a stay-at-home mom or a working mother, it often feels like there is little time to regroup and make sense of all the craziness.

In the midst of all of this, parenting can do a number on our confidence. We find ourselves doubting and questioning and second-guessing even the simplest decisions…all with the bottom line: Am I parenting well?

When my first child was born, I had *NO* experience with babies. I had never even babysat before! So…naturally, I knew exactly how everything would go, and *of course* it would all go perfectly.

Hmmm…

The Preparation

I quickly realized I had a lot to learn. I found myself asking God, "What am I supposed to do now?"

It seems like every new thing you bring home comes with a manual: your refrigerator, your cell phone, even your blender! I thought, *Why didn't God do that for us?* If my child had come with a manual the way a dishwasher does, I could have just flipped it open: *This is how they are wired; here are their special features; these are your child's gifts and talents. Here is a list of troubleshooting tips if things are not working well.* Oh yeah, and how about this one: *Here is the toll-free hotline number.* Now that I think about it, I'm not sure I've ever used one of those hotline numbers, but I sure would have used one for help with my baby!

When our first child was six months old, I began to search God's Word for everything it said about children. When she took naps, I studied parenting. When she went to bed at night, I studied some more! As it turns out, God *has* given us a manual on parenting. It is called The Bible.

My husband and I were pastoring at the time, and for weeks I taught a Bible Study to the mothers with young children. During those sessions, I taught them what I had learned that week… everything God had said in His Word, about how *He* intended parenting to work.

That was 29 years ago. Since that time, I have raised three children into adulthood, and I have taught school, worked in children's camps, worked in children's church, worked with pre-teen and teen groups, led teen mission trips, and done a whole lot more. And throughout all of this, I have discovered that the principles God helped me to see in those early days of parenting—the principles laid out in this book—absolutely *work*.

The principles revealed within these pages will not only place your children's feet on God's path—preparing them to both find their destinies and make right choices to fulfill these destinies—but they will also strengthen your family unit, creating an environment that will continually draw your family together, even as your children become teens and adults. And trust me when I say: There are few things more rewarding than raising children who make right choices, and who remain part of a cohesive "family" unit even into their adult years!

∽ *Thoughts for Action* ∽

- God has a vision for you as parents.
- The Bible is the "how to" manual for raising your children.
- When you follow God's plan for parenting, your children will bring you rest and delight!

For I know the thoughts and plans that I have for you, says the Lord, thoughts and plans for welfare and peace and not for evil, to give you hope in your final outcome.
                                                            Jeremiah 29:11

The Destination

*Successful parenting is:
Reaching the destination
God has for you!*

Parenting is full-time!

Oftentimes we begin to feel like, *I'll do whatever it takes to just make it through…and I'll figure it out as I go.* After all, parenting rarely looks like those nice pictures the parenting books paint!

There is a desire within every parent to reach that destination of 'successful parenting.' But actually getting there is another thing! My heart aches for families and the struggles parents experience. There are so many families who do not even know that something is missing, because the 'normal' has strayed so far from God's design. But let me tell you, it is never too late to turn things around!

One of the first steps toward that finish line of 'successful parenting' is realizing that God desires us to have more than just a nice family or good kids. Successful parenting is about accomplishing *God's design* for our family.

In order to reach this destination—*God's* destination for us—we must understand the importance of parenting with the BIG PICTURE in mind.

Imagine you are preparing to take a road trip to Disney World. (And to those of you who live close to Disney World and think you're off the hook, think again! *You'll* be taking a road trip to Disney *Land*.)

The first thing you need is a map (or, if you want to be technologically savvy, you can use some sort of GPS). Once you have that map or GPS, you need a *plan*. And once this BIG PICTURE framework is in place, and you've packed your luggage, you're ready to take off.

Now, for each of us, this journey will be different. For one thing, each of us begins from a different starting point. For another thing, each of us has a unique style of travel. Maybe your driver is practicing for NASCAR, and you have to beg them to stop so you don't wet your pants. Or maybe your driver feels that the joy is in the journey, and they pull over every time an opportunity for 'fun' pops up along the road.

No one can tell you exactly how this Disney World journey will go—after all, imagine what you would think if your neighbor started telling you *exactly* what would happen on your trip; even if they had taken the same trip, leaving from the exact same starting point and using the same map you planned to use, the two journeys would be entirely different! But by following the directions of the map, you will reach your destination.

Our children are the same way. We navigate from the passenger seat, and our child mans the driver's seat. Our job is to make sure they understand where they are going and how to get there.

The destination we are guiding them toward is the fulfillment of *God's design* for their life. In order to reach this destination, we need to keep the BIG PICTURE of parenting in mind—the map; the plan.

Each child comes with unique gifts and talents and potential, all packaged inside a tiny bundle—in other words, each child's *destination* is different. And this is where the metaphor breaks off.

While we can find Disney World with a map we bought at Wal-Mart, it's not so simple with our children. To find our child's destination, we cannot just toss a map into the shopping cart and bag it up with the celery! What we need is a map that shows us exactly where we are going for our child's *specific* destination. What turns do we make? What exits do we take? Where, exactly, are we headed…?

And this is where God's plan for our child's life comes into play. He has given us a map to follow, complete with the turns we should make and the exits we should take…the training, molding, and shaping that must take place. Once we see the BIG PICTURE, the journey begins to make a lot more sense.

~ Thoughts for Action ~

- Successful Parenting is about more than just having a "nice family" or "good kids."

- You need to see the BIG PICTURE in order to reach the destination God has set for you, your children, and your family.

- You are the navigator for your children, guiding them to the final destination God has planned for them!

...I am the Lord you God, Who teaches you to profit, Who leads you in the way that you should go.

Isaiah 48:17

The Journey

Parenting is a long journey,
so let's build in order to enjoy it!

Throughout my parenting journey, I learned the value of breaking big concepts down into smaller, more manageable servings. In the three points that follow—The What, The Why, and The How—we take spoonful-sized helpings to understand the BIG PICTURE goals of parenting.

The What: My job is to raise up children who can choose to listen to their spirits—children who know the difference between the voice of their flesh and the voice of their spirit, and who understand the war between the two.

The Why: You might have thought the 'why' was something like this: "To have good kids who won't embarrass me." But God has entrusted us with these arrows, and He wants to use them in the Kingdom for His glory. Each child is born with a purpose to fulfill—something that he/she is uniquely created for.

The How: Now comes 'the job'—and it will take all of the 18 years they live at home…and more!

Wherever you are in the timeline of raising your children, I want to encourage you that *the time is right.* You cannot rewind and go back a season (how we all wish we could!), but whatever you invest now will reap dividends in your future. Even if you started your journey driving the wrong way, it's never too late to change the directions you are providing for the driver. Turn them around, and get them heading toward their destination!

My heart's desire is that this book will help you be *proactive* instead of *reactive.*

> *Through skillful and Godly Wisdom is a house (a life, a home, a family) built, and by understanding it is established (on a sound and good foundation). By knowledge shall its chambers of every area be filled with all precious and pleasant riches.*
>
> Proverbs 24:3-4

This was what I always wanted—a home that was lovely both inside and out. And I found out that, through wisdom, I could build that. I could have a family established on a good and solid foundation! I could fill *every* area of my family's life with precious and pleasant riches. God said it was so!

And so the question became, how do I bring this to pass?

Remember, *parenting is a journey*! There's no need to start asking, "Are we there yet?" It's a long journey—you might as well choose to enjoy it!

~ *Thoughts for Action* ~

- *Our job as parents* is to raise children who can CHOOSE to listen to their spirits (children who can make *right choices!*).

- *The reason we do this* is to shape arrows God can use for His Kingdom.

- *We accomplish this by* following the parenting principles God has given us in His Word!

Through skillful and Godly Wisdom is a house (a life, a home, a family) **built,** *and by understanding it is established (on a sound and good foundation).*

Proverbs 23:3

THE PURPOSE

We Are Created by His Purpose and for His Purpose

Your children are marked for destiny.
Your children have a purpose.

s a child, I often posed these questions to my sister:

"Why are we here?"

"What are we supposed to do?"

At the time, I had no idea that I was actually asking, "What is my purpose?" But my little heart *knew* that I was part of something bigger than me.

Over the last decade, Rick Warren's *Purpose Driven Life* has sold more than 30 million copies—because people are looking for purpose!

Purpose Driven Life states, "Without a purpose, life is motion without meaning, activity without direction, and events without reason. Without a purpose, life is trivial, petty, and pointless."[1]

Cynthia Kersey's *Unstoppable Women* says, "94% of people have no defined purpose."[2] How horrible to experience the mechanical motion of living instead of the spark of aliveness that comes from a vision of purpose!

Children are created to carry a purpose. There are children who have come forth "by accident" and are unplanned by their parents, but they are not unplanned by God. While there are illegitimate parents, there are no illegitimate children!

Our children are marked for destiny. God has placed within each of them talents, gifts, strengths, and callings. God's design is that they will touch their world…that they will be *difference-makers*.

Now, you might ask, *Does that mean that all children are supposed to be missionaries and preachers?*

Absolutely not! God needs His love and His light shared on every path of life. He wants to tell *HIS STORY* through our children.

And as a parent, God has clearly defined a major purpose for *our* life. He is calling us to raise up part of the generation who—as

---

[1]Rick Warren, *Purpose Driven Life* (Zondervan, Grand Rapids, 2004), 30.
[2]Cynthia Kersey, *Unstoppable* (Rodale Books, Emmause, PA, 1 ed. 1998).

Daniel 11:32 says—knows their God and shall prove themselves strong, who shall stand firm and do exploits for Him.

God and Satan are in battle for our children. In the Forward of the book, *Battle for the Seed*, Myles Munroe gives us a BIG PICTURE view of why this battle is going on:

> "The power to change the future is with us in the present. God always goes after the seed within the fruit. In every seed, there is not just a tree but a forest. Have you noticed that whenever God wanted to fulfill His purpose He would give birth to a child?...Moses, Jacob, John Baptist, Jesus. And have you noticed that whenever Satan attempts to thwart God's purpose, he goes after the children…the next generation?"

> "Every nation is pregnant with a generation, and we all know that the condition of the mother affects the health of the baby. Whatever the mother eats, drinks, or inhales will be transferred to the offspring. In essence, the diet of the nation will manifest in the next generation."[3]

I Chronicles 12:32 tells us that, like the children of Issachar, we must have understanding of the times and the seasons in which we live and know what we ought to do. *We are the caretakers of God's seed and His plan.* He gave us children not only for our enjoyment and fulfillment, but for His purpose and plan. When we see the vision God has, we will take our place in 'the cause,' and we will impart that to our children.

---

[3] Patricia Morgan, *Battle for the Seed* (Whitaker, New Kingsington, PA; 2003), 8.

God has a Divine viewpoint He wants to show us. He wants us to see the view as He sees it so when we leave the highest point and walk in the day-to-days of life, that view will be imprinted on our hearts.

I once visited a beautiful property in Washington State that overlooks the Columbia River. The house is situated on top of a hill. The view from the BIG PICTURE window is breathtaking…

The majestic river snakes along at the bottom of the hill, and beyond the river is a cascade of rolling hills that extends to the horizon. There are horses in the pasture below and chickens in the fenced yard, next to the vegetable and flower garden. From the big window, I could see the river twisting off in both directions until it grew tiny in the distance. I could see the flowers that decorated the hills, blowing in a gentle breeze. My vision stretched for miles in all directions.

That picture is still imprinted in my mind these many years later. From the moment I saw the BIG PICTURE from that window, it was captured in my heart. Later, when I walked the pastures and picked my way through the garden, I experienced the details of the BIG PICTURE.

This is exactly what God wants to do in our heart. He wants to imprint the vision from that BIG PICTURE window. And when we are tending the gardens and the pastures in the day-to-day journey as a parent, we can pull back and recall what the BIG PICTURE view looks like, and we can make sure we are tending things according to the Master's plan.

~ Thoughts for Action ~

- Every child has a purpose. Every child is marked by God. This includes your children. *And this includes you!*

- You are the caretaker of God's seed and His plan!

- When you allow the BIG PICTURE to be imprinted on your memory, you can recall what it looked like as you go through the day-to-day journey of parenting.

For we are God's own handiwork (His workmanship), recreated in Christ Jesus, that we may do those good works which God predestined (planned beforehand) for us [taking paths which He prepared ahead of time], that we should walk in them [living the good life which He prearranged and made ready for us to live].

Ephesians 2:10

God's View Point

*The Bible says that your children are
a heritage, a blessing, a reward!*

One question we find ourselves asking is, *Who are these children God has given me?* Sometimes we ask this question when our daughter has climbed out of her crib early in the morning and retrieved her paints and paintbrushes from the top shelf of the closet and started creating her masterpiece on the floors, on the walls, and on her little brother. But we also ask this question when *little* things happen, or even when *nothing* is happening at all—when we just look at our children and wonder, *God, what am I supposed to be doing? Who are these children you have given me?*

The answer to this question, of course, can be found in God's Word! This is the view He wants you to see from the BIG PICTURE WINDOW:

God desired a godly offspring from your union.

Malachi 2:15

I and the children whom the Lord has given me are for signs and wonders. (Notice—the Lord has given!)

Isaiah 8:18

God has chosen, actually picked you out for Himself before the foundations of the world. That they should be holy (consecrated and set apart for Him) blameless in His sight. For He has foreordained you (destined you, planned in love for you) to be adopted and revealed as His own children thought Jesus Christ.

Ephesians 1: 4, 5

For You did form my inward parts; You did knit me together in my mother's womb. I will confess and praise You for You are fearful and wonderful and for the awful wonder of my birth! Wonderful are Your works, and that my inner self knows right well. My frame was not hidden from You when I was being formed in secret and intricately wrought (as if embroidered with various colors) in the depths of the earth. Your eyes saw my unformed substance and in your book all the days of my life were written before ever they took shape, when as yet thee was none of them.

Psalm 139:13 – 16

*Children are **a heritage** from the Lord.*
The fruit of the womb is a reward.
*Like **arrows** in the hand of a warrior*
So are the children of one's youth.

Psalm 127:3, 4 (emphasis added)

The Bible tells us that our children are a heritage, a blessing, a reward. But there is a shift in this particular verse…and the Bible also tells us that God calls our children arrows in the hand of a warrior…

∽ *Thoughts for Action* ∽

- God intends for your children to be a heritage, a blessing, and a reward for you…

- But God also intends for your children to be something greater!

- There is a level of comfort a warrior has knowing he has arrows in his pouch. We too sense a level comfort or satisfaction—knowing our arrows will be launched into our future.

That you may show yourselves to be blameless and guileless, innocent and uncontaminated, children of God without blemish (faultless, unrebukable) in the midst of a crooked and wicked generation [spiritually perverted and perverse], among whom you are seen as bright lights shining out clearly in the dark world.

Philippians 2:15

Like Arrows in the Hand of a Warrior

*You should see purpose
when you see your children.
You should see destiny.*

An arrow in the hand of a warrior is his weapon for war. Why does God refer to our children as weapons? Does that seem odd? Because He desires our children to be *"Dangerous for Good."* He desires that His arrows go swift and far, to penetrate the world and advance the Gospel, causing great damage to the kingdom of darkness. Our children are the arrows that God is launching *into the future*. He has paired each of them with talents, abilities, and personality traits—all to fit the design He has for them. When we connect with God's unique plan for our children and train them accordingly, they are certain to travel far.

A lesson in arrows that parallels God's plan for our children:

- Arrows formed from wood require time, skill, and care to fashion so that they remain tempered, strong, stable, and sharp—able to fly far.

- Every arrow has a shaft that is hardened—usually in a slow fire.

- The spine is strong, with little bend when compressed.

- Different arrows have different purposes. Some are stronger, shorter, and sturdier. Others are lightweight and well-balanced. Some are intended to fly a long distance with great accuracy, while others are designed for close range—intended to do great damage.

- The head of the arrow determines its purpose—the shape dependent upon what that arrow must penetrate.

- The fletching at the back is the stabilizer of flight.

- The nock is where the arrow fits into the bow—it keeps the arrow in place as the bow is drawn back.

- And of course, there is the bow! The bow launches the arrows…and who do you think the bow represents? That's right—the bow represents the parents! The bow must be strong and stable, not wobbly or weak, and this will allow the arrows to launch out into the world, flying as far as they were meant to fly

We see a beautiful picture drawn here, with the parallel between the forming, fashioning, and purpose of arrows and the forming, fashioning, and purpose of *God's* arrows—our children! Maybe you thought you were just going to be a soccer mom or a baseball coach, but even as you are cutting up those oranges for the soccer games or coaching your kid's baseball games, you are fashioning arrows for God.

As a parent, you need to learn to see your children the way *God* sees your children…

When you see your children, you should see *purpose*. When you see your children, you should see *destiny*.

~ *Thoughts for Action* ~

- God desires for your children to be *Dangerous for Good*!
- Your children are like arrows, and each of them is designed for a specific purpose.
- When you connect with God's plan for each of your children, they will travel far!

Many plan are in a man's mind, but it is the Lord's purpose for him that will stand.
Proverbs 19:21

Difference

*Recognize strengths,
and recognize weaknesses too!*

God made each of us to be different, with different gifts, different temperaments, and different personalities.

I Corinthians 12:12-18 tells us that God knit the church together with all its various parts arranged and functioning together. Our family is the same way—each person is different, with different strengths and weakness, because we are made to fit *together*.

Even though it sometimes feels like the world would be a much better place if everyone would just get their act together and be exactly like us(!), our family would be an absolute mess if we were all the same. It isn't an accident how God put our families together—with different personalities, strengths, and weaknesses under one roof. This is all part of His plan, and it is important to accentuate the differences and celebrate the strengths!

When our children were in elementary school, we had a junior Olympics at school. Throughout the week, my son was winning everything, and by the end of the week he had a small mountain of 'gold medals' stacked in his room.

That same week, my oldest daughter tried with all her heart to win something, but when the week ended her hands were still empty. She came to me crying and expressing how disappointed she was. "He got so many, and I didn't even get one!"

Of course, I could have said to her, "Well, baby, that's life." I could have said, "Try harder next time," or "Rejoice with those who rejoice."

Instead, I used that moment to separate strengths. "Yes," I said, "I know. He is very good at sports, and that might not be your greatest strength." But then, I reminded her of what had happened the previous weekend…

On that weekend, our family had gone to minister at a small church so the pastors could take a vacation. My husband was going to preach the service, and my oldest daughter and I were going to do the children's service. In the days leading up to that Sunday, she and I prepared a lesson, and we went over our material until we felt that we were ready. But when we arrived at the church on Sunday morning…I couldn't find my prepared material anywhere! I turned to my daughter, and I asked her if she would be able to just flow with me. Her answer? Emphatically, "Yes!"

Before I knew it, the kids had arrived, and my daughter had found a clown costume in the prop room and put it on, and she began a Scripture Game with the children! After that, we adlibbed a puppet show—we knew the direction we were going, but we had no script—and she was absolutely amazing! The whole service went just like this. She was only in the 5th grade, but her age didn't deter her at all! I would go to the back to get the next thing ready, and she would be out front with the children playing a game or teaching an object lesson. Then I would teach, and she would go to the back and get another object lesson ready.

The funny thing? When church ended, my planned material showed up…all of a sudden! It was as though the Holy Spirit was saying, "I just wanted to show the two of you that you could do it without the materials."

When my daughter came to me crying on the day of the junior Olympics award ceremony, I told her, "There were no medals given out last Sunday after church. There were no medals given out when you used your gifts and talents and just stepped in and flowed with me and ministered to those children. But if Jesus was giving out medals for that day, I know that you would have gotten all the gold medals!" This changed her perspective. She realized, she was talented also! Her talents were just in different areas.

Train up a child in the way that he should go [and in accordance with his individual gifts or bent], and when he is old he will not depart from it.

Proverbs 22:6

When we discover the gifts and bents of our children and begin to steer them *in the way that they should go*, why *would* they depart? When they have found the pulse of who they are created to be, why would they *want* to chase after something else?

When my children were still small, I began to recognize and pull out each of their strengths. I helped them build on these strengths, and I saw peace in my children as they accepted and celebrated their own unique strengths *as well as* their siblings' unique strengths…instead of comparing and feeling threatened.

I also began to recognize each child's weaknesses, and I helped them to see these weaknesses as well.

After all, weaknesses are not to be ignored. They are called weaknesses, not failures! While the natural reaction to a 'weakness' is often to treat it as an *icky something* that should be hidden in the back of a closet, a healthy approach in dealing with your child's weak areas is to point out, "This is not a strong area in your life, and so we need to be aware of it. It might never become a *strong area*, but as we learn how to approach it, we can work to improve it!"

While God gave my oldest daughter an overflow of talents when it comes to working with children, her college degree in early childhood education required more than just prodigious skills in understanding and interacting with kids…it required a whole bunch of math courses! Sure, the math courses were difficult for her. Some courses she had to retake, though she gave it her all. Sure, they seemed pointless! But instead of complaining or giving up, she pressed through. Ecclesiastes 3:5 says, "For a dream comes with much business and painful effort." These days, she is using her gifts and talents as an elementary teacher, training her children to make right choices—and she even had the opportunity to spend three years teaching elementary school on the mission field! She was able to reach these goals because she understood: Sometimes you have to confront your weaknesses in order to use your strengths. When you do this, the reward is great!

∽ *Thoughts for Action* ∽

- God created each member in your family to be different… so that they will fit together!

- Accentuate differences.

- Acknowledge weaknesses.

- Celebrate strengths!

For You did form my inward parts; You did knit me together in my mother's womb. I will confess and praise You for You are fearful and wonderful and for the awful wonder of my birth! Wonderful are Your works, and that my inner self knows right well. My frame was not hidden from You when I was being formed in secret and intricately and curiously wrought [as if embroidered with various colors] in the depths of the earth. Your eyes saw my unformed substance, and in Your book all the days of my life were written before ever they took shape.

Psalm 139: 13-16

OUR ROLE AS A PARENT

You are Important and Extremely Significant

*God gave you these children,
and you are suited for the job!*

Oftentimes when we think of parenting, our focus turns to the discipline aspects of raising children. However, if we want to get results that really work, there are important steps before we get to discipline. Discipline is NOT the foundation; something else comes first. In the parenting process, *you* come first. Who *you* are matters!

One of the biggest things to understand about parenting is this: It is important to **believe in yourself**. You are *anointed by God* to be a parent! Whether your children are strong-willed (and you are not), or whether your children are shy (and you are outgoing), or whether there is *anything at all* that makes it seem like you are not suited to be the parent of your child, you must remember that you are anointed by God to be a parent! God did not make a mistake. He has put your family together, and you are perfectly designed and fashioned and fit to lead it. *You have what it takes.* Settle that now.

Outward circumstances do not make us who we are. What we believe in our heart makes us who we are. Unfortunately, our current culture has misled our thinking, so that we think, "When I get married, I will feel different," or, "When I become a parent, I will be different." The variations on this thinking are endless—*When I get this job*, or *When I reach this certain age*, or *When I fill-in-the-blank*, I will change.

When I became a mother, I dealt with a lot of insecurities. This came from a childhood in which I grew up feeling insecure, and although I had made huge strides in correcting my thinking, the sudden transition into "Mama" pulled these insecurities back to the surface—fast! I wasn't sure if I was doing the job right. I wasn't even sure if I could!

Shortly after my first daughter was born—she was about four weeks old at the time—I went to the mall with a friend of mine… whose baby was four months old. Now, of course, there is quite a difference between a four *week* old baby and a four *month* old baby. Right? I mean, anyone in their right mind would know that! But while we were out, I noticed that my friend's baby girl was smiling and interacting with the world. Meanwhile, my baby girl wasn't doing any of this! She wasn't smiling, she wasn't cooing, she wasn't interacting with strangers…

What is wrong with my baby! Does my friend's baby like her more than my baby likes me? What am I doing wrong? Is her baby smarter than mine? My baby is just lying there in her stroller doing nothing!

It's absurd, I know. But it's what the devil does to us! He preys on our weaknesses and wants to move into our thinking. It's important to for us to catch and get a hold of "who we really are"—because…

Much of what our children learn will be *caught* rather than *taught*!

My dad used to always joke around and say, "Do as I say, not as I do." But as we journey along the road of parenting, we must understand that it does not work like this!

I remember when my one of my daughters was 3 years old and I was directing a church Christmas production. It was a small church, and so we were including all the children—from my 3-year-old all the way up to the 16-year-olds (of course, my 3-year-old could not understand why I had cast a teenager to play Mary, instead of casting her!).

Now, when I am directing a play, I often sound like a broken record. "I don't hear you!" "Slow down." "Do it again." I love watching children perform—but I always feel disappointed if the actors mumble their lines or rush through their parts, looking like they would rather be somewhere else (which, of course, might be the case!). The actors might know their lines and staging perfectly, but the audience only gets one chance to catch the story. After all, there is no rewind button for the audience.

So there you go—picture yourself in my position, trying to make sure a bunch of "actors" between the ages of three and 16 speak loudly and slowly and with perfect enunciation. You can understand that perhaps I was a bit relentless. A bit…harsh.

At some point during this process, I passed by the living room one afternoon to see my daughter playing "Christmas Play Rehearsal." She had her stuffed animals lined up, with a pen behind her ear and a clipboard in her hand. I watched her, and I witnessed…her rendition of me! I was loud. I was bossy. I was demanding. And I was very repetitive. It was a startling reflection of what I looked and sounded like to my daughter. Sure, the Christmas production went well…but she "caught" something from me I did want her to learn. I wonder if I could have gotten the same result and been a better *model*.

So many girls grow up wanting to be a model, and they don't realize that when they become a parent…a model is *exactly* what they become. Every day, you are on the runway, showing your children how to wear their life.

There is an often-used quote attributed to St. Francis of Assisi that goes like this: "Preach the gospel at all times; when necessary, use words."

This same principle applies to parenting! We are training our children not only with the words we speak to them, but with everything we do. They learn how to live by watching us every day, by witnessing the examples we set through authority, victory, love, patience, giving, submission, purity of heart, attitude, peacefulness, discipline, order and neatness, honesty, and everything else. Every day, we show our children what it looks like to be "grown up." Children watch everything; they catch more than we think. It is true—we become a product of our environment. That is exactly why I think of myself as "An Environmentalist"—always remaining sharply conscious of the environment in my home. I am *protective* of it. It is my job, as a parent, to control the environment and set the thermostat where it needs to be.

If you find yourself wondering why your kids are not acting the way you "feel that they should," it might be time to break out the old checklist of self-evaluation:

- ☐ How is my attitude? Do my children see a rebellious attitude in me?

- ☐ Am I acting one way in public and another way at home?

- ☐ What do I do if I do not get my way, or if things are not going well for me?

- ☐ Do my children witness my relationship with God as a 'normal' part of everyday living…or is it private and saved for Sundays or special occasions?

- ☐ Do I mean what I say?

- ☐ Do I walk in integrity and strong character?

- ☐ Am I honest with everyone?

- ☐ Do I make excuses for myself and my behavior?

- ☐ Do I blame others when things go wrong?

You are the model…and your children will follow your example. If they are catching something you don't like, you might need to make some changes yourself.

Become an environmentalist! Take care of the example your children are seeing daily, and set the thermostat in your home to where you want it to be.

∽ Thoughts for Action ∽

- You are important. *The person who you are matters.*

- Remember: you are anointed by God to be a parent. Believe in yourself!

- Outward circumstances do not make you who you are. *What you believe in your heart* makes you who you are!

- Much of what your children learn will be *caught* rather than *taught*!

- You are a model. Every day, you are on the runway, showing your children how to wear their life. What a self-improvement program parenting can be.

- Becoming a parent doesn't change the inward view we have of ourselves; it only ends up accentuating it.

You are Important and Extremely Significant

Let no one despise or think less of you because of your youth, be an example (pattern) for the believers in **speech**, *in* **conduct**, *in* **love**, *in* **faith**, *and in* **purity**.

1 Timothy 4:12

Job Description: Mom

*Parenting is a job,
and not for the weak at heart!*

When you are working in the business world, you are given a job description. If you were working on a job and you were busy all day, every day, but did not accomplish your job description and did not produce what you were hired to do, something would have to be adjusted.

God has a job description for us as parents. Before we can effectively train our children, we must see how He defines our job. Effective parenting goes way beyond the rules and standards we desire. It is imperative to see who your seed is according to God's Word. But it is also important to see who God says you are, since you are a major player in His plans for your child. If we understand what God desires in us, as parents, our children will be the fruit of our lives.

Proverbs 127:3 says the fruit of your womb a reward.

Here is a job description that is funny, but it holds a lot of truth. Perhaps if we had read this before we "signed up" for being a mother, we might have changed our minds!

Job Description:
Mom, Mommy, Mama, Mother, Ma

Long-term team players needed for challenging permanent work in an often chaotic environment. Candidates must possess excellent communication and organizational skills and be willing to work variable hours, which will include evenings and weekends and frequent 24-hour shifts on call.

Some overnight travel required, including trips to primitive camping sites on rainy weekends and endless sports tournaments in faraway cities. Travel expenses not reimbursed. Extensive courier duties also required.

Responsibilities:

Must provide on-the-site training in basic life skills, such as nose-blowing and shoe tying.

Must have strong skills in negotiating, conflict resolution, and crisis management. Ability to suture flesh wounds a plus.

Must be able to think outside of the box but not lose track of the box, because you most likely will need it for a school project. Must reconcile petty cash disbursements and be proficient in managing budgets and resources fairly, unless you want to hear, "He got more than me!" for the rest of your life.

Also, must be able to drive motor vehicle safely under loud and adverse conditions while simultaneously practicing above-mentioned skills in conflict resolution. Must be able to choose your battles and stick to your guns. Must be able to withstand criticism, such as, "You don't know anything."

Must be willing to be hated at least temporarily, until someone needs $5 to go skating.

Must be willing to bite tongue repeatedly. Also, must possess the physical stamina of a pack mule and be able to go from zero to 60mph in three seconds flat in case, this time, the screams from the backyard are not someone just crying wolf.

Must be willing to face stimulating technical challenges, such as small gadget repair, mysteriously sluggish toilets and stuck zippers.

Must screen phone calls, maintain calendars, and coordinate production of multiple homework projects.

Must have ability to plan and organize social gatherings for clients of all ages and mental outlooks.

Must handle assembly and product safety testing of a half million cheap, plastic toys and battery operated devices.

Also, must have a highly energetic entrepreneurial spirit, because fund-raiser will be your middle name.

Must have a diverse knowledge base, so as to answer questions such as, "What makes the wind move?" or, "Why can't they just go in and shoot Saddam Hussein?" on the fly.

Must always hope for the best but be prepared for the worst. Must assume final, complete accountability for the quality of the end product.

Responsibilities also include floor maintenance and janitorial work throughout the facility.

Possibility for Advancement and Promotion:

Virtually none. Your job is to remain in the same position for years, without complaining, constantly retraining and updating your skills, so that those in your charge can ultimately surpass you.

Previous Experience:

None required, unfortunately. On-the-job training offered on a continually exhausting basis.

Wages and Compensation:

You pay them, offering frequent raises and bonuses. A balloon payment is due when they turn 18 because of the assumption that college will help them become financially independent. When you die, you give them whatever is left.

The oddest thing about this reverse-salary scheme is that you actually enjoy it and wish you could only do more.

Benefits:

While no health or dental insurance, no pension, no tuition reimbursement, no paid holidays, and no stock options are offered, the job supplies limitless opportunities for personal growth and free hugs for life if you play your cards right.

Source unknown

Sure, this is funny. But…it's also true! Parenting *is* a job. God gave it to us. And as with any job, our Boss has expectations for our job performance. As a parent, we have to make sure the Main Thing remains the Main Thing. With all that screams for our attention (and oh, can it scream!), at the end of the day we can check in with our Boss and see if we need to make some adjustments. It doesn't matter if I am pleased with the way that something went, but if God is pleased.

∽ *Thoughts for Action* ∽

- Parenting can be great fun…
- …but it is also a job!

"Your children are not your hobby, they are your calling. Cherish the children who share your name.[4]"

~Max Lucado

---

[4] Max Lucado, *Facing Your Giants* (Thomas Nelson Publishers, Nashville, TN; 2006), 157.

How Can We Do This Job?

Realize that you will make mistakes…
When you make them, repent and move forward!

We Need Confidence!

Two of the greatest weapons the enemy uses against parents are **intimidation and guilt**.

Have you heard conversations like this in your head:

"What do you think you are doing?"

"You are such a _____! What makes you think can _____?"

That voice in my head used to say stuff like this: "…And you're teaching parenting classes? What a joke! Your kids got into strife today. You got upset with them…and *you're* teaching *others* about parenting?"

Satan's schemes are designed to zap us of our confidence and authority as a parent. To intimidate is *to render timid, inspire feelings of fear, and to discourage.* When we are intimidated, we end up feeling inadequate. We begin to doubt our ability to parent effectively. Intimidation changes our focus from *others* to *ourselves*, and we begin to feel inferior, discouraged, and confused. We lose our perspective. And then, instead of dealing with the root of intimidation—which is fear—we react to the way we feel, therefore coming into agreement with our enemy.

Now, what about guilt! Oh, that guilt record can sure play loud and clear, can't it?

"You didn't do enough! You didn't pray enough, play enough. You weren't sensitive enough!"

Early on in my parenting journey, I found that Satan was always telling me I hadn't done *this* enough, or I hadn't done *that* enough. Or else, I hadn't done this or that *well* enough. I wasn't being the parent I wanted to be. I had fallen short in so many different ways…

And then one night, I decided that I'd had enough. "That's not true!" I said.

Deep down in my heart, I felt the Holy Spirit say, "Well, it's about time!"

Remember, Satan *wants* you to abdicate your authority. He wants to regain the power Jesus stripped from him. He wants you to doubt who you are and where you are going.

When my children were pre-school age, I was having praise and worship and Bible time with them. They were distracted and really not paying attention. I was getting frustrated and really did not know what to do. I asked the Lord, "Do I make them praise You and pray? I don't want to force them; I want it to come from their hearts."

Sitting right there on the kitchen floor with 3 uncooperative children, He spoke to my spirit and said, "Do you make them brush their teeth?" I got it. Yes! Yes, I make them brush their teeth, because I am training them. That was my answer. I was training my children in the way they should go.

Our spirit wants to praise, but if the flesh is busy and distracted, it can steer any of us away from what our spirit wants to do. That day helped me a lot with my confidence. I knew, "I am called to train them in the way they should go."

There are times you will hear clearly what to do. But there are many times you might not be sure. It seems there are a lot more of those time…when you are just not sure what to do. I learned as I trusted God with my parenting and stepped out to be the leader, He caused me to grow in following Him. The Holy Spirit inside you is your guide. If you will have confidence in yourself to do the job, you will use the tools God has graced you with. If you make a mistake, know that God will make it clear to you. Many times, as the children were in bed, I would have a sense that God was talking to me about adjustments I needed to make in my parenting approach. Sometimes, it would be necessary to apologize to the children the next morning and let them know that God showed me I was not listening to my spirit and had made a wrong choice in parenting them. It is so precious to model walking with Jesus to our children. It is not a perfect walk, but a sweet and humble walk. What better way to model for them the Christ life.

As you trust God and follow Jesus, you will grow in the confidence and in the anointing God has given you to parent.

Sure, we'll make mistakes as parents. We'll make mistakes in *every* area of life, because we are human. But this is no reason to feel guilty! If you make a mistake, admit it. Repent to God. Repent to your children. And keep moving forward!

∽ *Thoughts for Action* ∽

- Satan will try to use intimidation and guilt against you; he wants to strip you of your authority.

- Be bold! Be the parent! Be a *follower of Jesus*!

- You will make mistakes as a parent—every parent does!

- The question is not whether you make a mistake; the question is how you handle it. When you make a mistake, acknowledge it. Repent to God. Repent to your children. And move on!

> *...I may hear this of you; that you are standing firm in united spirit and purpose, striving side by side and contending with a single mind for the faith of the Gospel. And do not for a moment be frightened or intimidated in anything by your*

opponents and adversaries, for such constancy and fearlessness will be a clear sign to them of their impending destruction, but a sure token and evidence of your deliverance and salvation, and that from God.

Philippians 1:27b-28

A Vision

*Your child has been born into destiny.
Keep this vision in mind!*

As the light of parenting gets filtered through the prism of our desire to be the best parent in the world, it becomes easy to lose sight of the reason for this light: the stewardship God gave us! Sure, we want to have a great family; we want to have memorable vacations; we want our kids to be well-educated and to marry a great spouse and to be happy. But there is more to parenting than this. God has given us an assignment. A purpose. A *vision*.

> *Where there is no vision, the people perish.*
> Proverbs 29:18

Let's make sure we understand exactly *why* vision is so vital…

It is often easy as a parent to feel weary, exhausted, stressed, distracted…tired of doing the same things over and over again. It is natural to feel this way whether you have vision or not. But *when you have vision,* it is also easy to continue pressing forward, because you know that God has entrusted you with destinies.

In *Battle for Our Seed*, Patricia Morgan says the following:

> *We are incubating the next generation of leaders. This generation brooding is angry, confused, desensitized, rebellious, and immoral. We have in our hands the future leaders of our nation. It is in our hands to change the future. We must protect and preserve it. Our number one job to educate for eternity. If we merely provide a "safe place" then we are not equipping world changers. God has not called us to a holy huddle. He is not calling us to somehow preserve our seed, defend our children, and keep them off of and out of the world. He is calling us to raise up a generation who know that they are called with a mandate on their lives and to take the kingdom of this world by force. It doesn't matter what life has dished out to them so far. It hasn't changed the call of God on their lives.*[5]

We must be relentless in preserving our children for God. In this information age where knowledge is at the fingertips of practically every man, woman, and child, we must be aware of the values and messages being inserted into our family.

Perhaps we need to think more like dynasties think. They have a *vision*. They know why their children are born: They are born into destiny. They are born as heirs to a throne. They are molded and shaped in a certain way, and they are pointed in the directions they are destined to go.

---

[5] Patricia Morgan, *Battle for the Seed* (Whitaker, New Kingsington, PA; 2003).

A boy born into a dynasty—born to be a future king—is fashioned daily to fulfill his predetermined call. He is daily *made aware of* his destiny—raised to be superior, a leader, a person of privilege, born for a purpose. There are certain things he does not do, activities he does not participate in. Not because he can't, but because he has a destiny and a purpose in view.

And so it should be with our children! We need to have a similar kind of vision. Just as heirs to a throne are molded and shaped a certain way, we as parents are shaping this next generation…forming arrows to be launched by God.

Parenting is not just a fun and rewarding experience—although it certainly *is* that—but it is also a job. God wants you to prepare your children for their launch! And the way you do this is by being the Gatekeeper and the Trainer…

～ *Thoughts for Action* ～

You should *daily* make your children aware of their destinies!

- You should *daily* parent with your children's destinies in mind!
- You are preparing children who are heirs to the Kingdom of God.
- Though every child has a destiny, not every child has been made aware of it. Oftentimes, a child's environment

makes it difficult to tap into purpose because what he sees and hears is contrary to what he has been created for.

...that they may be called oaks of righteousness, [lofty, strong, and magnificent, distinguished for uprightness, justice, and right standing with God], the planting of the Lord, that He may be glorified.

Isaiah 61:3b

Gatekeeper

*Your child's body is a temple of the Holy Spirit...
and you are the gatekeeper of this temple!*

The gatekeeper is spoken of in I Chronicles 9:17-27. The gatekeepers were the men who stood at the entrances and the threshold to the temple. They were in charge of the chambers and the treasury of the House of God. Their job was to make sure nothing holy was taken from the treasury, and to make sure nothing unholy was brought through the gates.

When Jesus was crucified, the temple veil was torn in two—signifying the shift from the Old Covenant to the New Covenant. In the New Covenant, the temple was no longer a man-made structure, but was, instead, us as individuals.

> *Do you not know that your **body is the temple of the Holy Spirit** Who lives with in you, Whom you have received as a Gift from God.*
>
> I Corinthians 6:19

God has entrusted *us* as the gatekeepers over our children. And as they grow older, we must train them to become the gatekeepers themselves—to know how to guard their treasury, so that nothing holy is removed, and so that nothing unholy is allowed entrance.

It is easy to recognize our role as gatekeepers in the visible, natural manner of speaking—guarding our children, shielding them from danger, and training them to protect themselves from these dangers. But we need to become as alert and proactive in protecting their inner treasury—guarding their eye gates; guarding their ear gates; remaining sharply aware of what we allow to enter into their temple and settle down in their heart.

As parents, we are not trying to keep our children "out of" and "off of" things—we are not giving them an "I can't" Gospel, nor are we training them in a fear-based manner of thought—but rather, we are making sure that they understand the importance of guarding their heart. They are children of destiny and great purpose and vision. Our job is to provide oversight of their hearts as we teach them to do the same.

A lot of children make "right" choices (for a while) because "Mom and Dad say so," or because "teachers say so," or because someone is watching. Many children (and adults) behave well with external restraints in place. If a child only complies when "someone is watching" – only when external expectations are in place, there is no maturing process in the areas of personal responsibility. They are not getting to practice how to govern themselves. Often times we see this point collide in college when so much external control has been lifted. We must train our children to make right choices when they are young. In this way, we raise up children who will not "see what they can get away with," but who will instead police themselves, becoming the gatekeepers of God's temples.

When my older daughter was in kindergarten, she was at a friend's house and they were about to watch some animated show on television. My daughter asked to call home. She wanted to know if that particular show would be okay for her to watch. Later, the mother said to me, "Wow, you have your children well-trained." She thought my daughter was calling for permission to watch the show...but in fact, she was calling to see if it would be good for her spirit to watch it. At 5 years old, she was already gaining an understanding of and assuming responsibility for guarding her heart. This is what it means to protect the treasuries of the heart!

On another occasion, my younger daughter was playing with a friend outside. Her friend wanted to share a juicy story about a movie she had seen. My daughter told the girl, "No, I don't want to hear it."

The friend insisted.

Again, my daughter said, "No, I don't want to hear it."

"Oh, it's not that bad!" the friend said, and she began to tell the story.

At this point, I looked out the window to see my daughter... running toward the house with her ears covered—loud noises pouring out of her mouth! When she came inside, I asked her what in the world was going on.

She said she did not want to hear what her friend had to say, because it was something that was not going to be good for her spirit.

They had grasped the vision! They did not live in an "I can't" Gospel or an "I am not allowed to" family. They understood that inside them was a precious treasure that God had deposited. They knew God had a wonderful destiny for them to discover. They understood that the enemy will always try to sow bad seeds…but they could guard their hearts against it. They were grasping the concept that they had something valuable to protect.

How do we instill this? When children understand who they really are—*the real them is a spirit, who lives in an earth suit*—it is simple.

This becomes more and more challenging as children grow older and the pull of the world becomes stronger. As they walk deeper into their independence, it is easy for them to become drawn by what is the 'norm'—by what is 'cool' or 'popular.' It is *not* always easy to guard the treasures of the heart, but the earlier you start training them, the better-equipped they will be!

When you keep your children focused on your role as a gatekeeper, it gives them a larger perspective of their life. Often I would say, "I am the gatekeeper, honey. I am doing my job." It helped them focus on destiny, and it put today's challenges into perspective. Today is important, of course. But today is not *the most* important!

As parents with purpose, we need discernment regarding the movies, television shows, and books our children consume. We need to be aware of who they are friends with. We need to monitor what our children are feeding on—what is entering the gates of the temple.

Whatever is in the heart is what we will think. What we think is what we become.

As parents, we hold the reins. We let out the reins to give our children more freedom…and we pull back on the reins if we see that they are not handling the freedom well. As a gatekeeper, we don't stand by and say, "Oh well." NO! We make adjustments. We monitor. And we always instill within our children the BIG PICTURE, the *vision*, so that when they become the sole gatekeeper of their temple, they will be able to guard it well.

~ *Thoughts for Action* ~

- Your child's body is the temple of the Holy Spirit—and your job is to guard this temple.

- Train your children to recognize the importance of guarding their temple, and teach them to guard their temple on their own. They have something valuable to protect.

- We do not live in an "I can't" Gospel. We live with an understanding of the value of our temples!

- Today is important. But today is not the *most important*.

Keep and guard your heart with all vigilance and above all that you guard, and above all that you guard, for out of it flows the springs of life.

Proverbs 4:23

Trainer

A great coach prepares their team to win.
A great parent does the same thing.

My older daughter did not enjoy team sports. After T-ball, she decided that team sports were just plain *not for her*.

Growing up, however, she found that she could race the boys her age…and beat them. She also found that this was cool! So when she reached high school, she joined the track team. It seemed like a great idea to her…until after the first couple sessions.

The coach in charge had no mercy. He knew what he wanted—he wanted to see these young people reach their potential. He saw *beyond* the present; he was Future Focused.

My daughter wanted to quit, but as much as I hated driving her to track practice every Tuesday and Thursday while she cried and pled her case, my husband and I felt it was important for her to learn this lesson in perseverance.

Her coach was not moved by anything. The kids whined when he made them do pushups in the mud. When this failed to affect him in any way, they snarled at him while they did sit ups with worms by their heads. They complained when he pushed them to run much further than they thought they could run. But none of this moved him. His goal was not to *be liked*; his goal was to produce results.

In the end, my daughter grew in ways she never even knew she needed to grow.

It took someone who saw past the present, someone who pushed her to break barriers she did not even know were blocking her, for her to uncover the potential inside. This is a trainer's job, a coach's job: to see potential; to see beyond the present to the future. A great coach implements a great game plan, drawing up plays and formations they believe will work against the opponent. A great coach gives out assignments based on strengths. A great coach inspires and motivates.

A great coach corrects mistakes, drills the basics, keeps players conditioned, and through it all they inspire confidence. This is the mindset a parent must have. So many parents hope so desperately to *be liked* by their children, and therefore, they forgo the often hard and uncomfortable process of training. It is so much easier to 'keep the peace,' 'take the path of least resistance,' and 'be approved of.' But we must remember we are given stewardship to train. Like a coach is hired to produce results with a team, we are under God's command *to train our children in the way they should go and in keeping with their individual bents.*

In the spirit, we want our children to say, "Look at these abs; check out my muscles! Look how far I can run."

Do you not know that in a race all the runners compete, but only one receives the prize? So run your race that you may lay hold of the prize and make it yours.

Now every athlete who goes into training conducts himself temperately and restricts himself in all things. They do it to win a wreath that will soon wither, but we do it to receive a crown of eternal blessedness that cannot wither.

Therefore I do not run uncertainly without definite aim. I do not box like one beating the air and striking without an adversary.

But like a boxer I buffet my body (handle it roughly, discipline it by hardships) and subdue it, for fear that after proclaiming to others the Gospel and things pertaining to it, I myself should become unfit and not stand the test of time, be unapproved and rejected as a counterfeit.

I Corinthians 9:24-27

Without the mindset of a trainer, you may compromise your vision when the waters grow turbulent, when the knots of anxiousness twist your stomach. It is easy to back down, to take a less turbulent road. But remember: many of the choices we make in parenting have both pain and pleasure. If we choose to follow the high road (God's highest and best path), there is pain in pressing through that initial pressure, but on the other side we will find victory, freedom, and enlargement. Oftentimes, our flesh must go through a difficult process. But the pleasure is eternal, and is well worth the temporary pain.

On the other hand, we can choose the easier road—the road of "making things smoother right now." This might allow for immediate pleasure, peace, and ease—and the flesh likes it…for now. But on the other side of this process is sorrow, enslavement, loss, and unending sorrow.

If we think like a trainer, conditioning our children and stretching them to the next level for the race of life, our focus will be long term. This makes it much easier to conquer difficult decisions in the present. After all, we are preparing our children for life. Sure, the Olympics are important. The Super Bowl is fun. But nothing is more important than the task we are shaping our children for—to *find* their course, *run* their course, and *finish* their course with joy!

∽ *Thoughts for Action* ∽

- As a parent, you are in place to *produce results*.

- Parent with the mindset of a trainer!

- Taking the road of "least resistance" in parenting feels good for now…but it will leave you with sorrow in the long run.

The road to Life is a disciplined Life; ignore correction and you're lost for good.

                                        Proverbs 10:17 Message

LAYING THE FOUNDATION
UPON WHICH TO BUILD

Build for the Future...by Making a Strong Foundation

*In order for a building to stand,
a strong foundation must be laid.*

When I visited the National Cathedral in Washington, D.C., I felt absolutely awed by the impressive building: the huge doors, the beautiful spires, the majestic stained glass windows and exquisite material. The place is massive; breathtaking. But what holds that whole place together?

That's right—it is *the foundation*!

No one gawks at the huge blocks the cathedral is built upon. No one whips out the camera to capture images and memories of the foundation. Everyone who visits the building looks up, admiring the beauty that stretches toward Heaven. But without the building's strong foundation, there would be nothing to admire.

Several years ago, we had a neighbor at the bottom of our street who was adding a room onto their house. For months, the occasional truck and the intermittent noise of a construction crew buzzed around an ugly hole in the ground, surrounded by an orange, plastic fence. Sometimes, we saw a new dirt pile. Otherwise, nothing much happened. Most days, everything looked quite boring. The whole thing looked messy. We quit paying attention. And then, one day, we drove down our hill and the walls were up! We were shocked.

When we returned home that day, the walls were paired with windows and a roof. Just like that!

The construction crew spent a lot of time on that "messy, in the trenches" stuff, laying the foundation that made it look to all the world as though nothing much was happening. And this is exactly what parenting is like!

Sure, we want to put the walls up. We want to throw the roof on top. But without a solid foundation, the walls and roof will crumble.

So far in this book, we have been learning to lay the foundation—learning to see the BIG PICTURE and build accordingly. We have learned to catch sight of what God has in mind for the children He has given us, to understand what He sees as our purpose and role in parenting.

Building a foundation is the least exciting thing about building. It is messy—unimpressive to the normal bystander—and…well, it can seem quite boring. The foundation is a lot of labor-drudgery type of work. But you cannot think about putting up walls and hanging pictures on the walls until the dirt has been dug and the foundation laid.

> *And let us not lose heart and grow weary and faint in acting noble and doing right, for in due time and at the appointed season we shall reap, if we do not loosen and relax our courage and faint.*
>
> Galatians 6:9

Although foundation work is messy—although it often seems we are making little or no progress—you will one day look at your children and realize, all of a sudden, that they are grown! Independence is approaching. The walls are going up, and the roof will soon join it. Our job as parents is to make sure the foundation work is done well, so that the structure is set on solid and firm ground and will be able to stand on its own.

Notice that when Jesus told the parable of the foolish man who built his house upon the sand, He never said *if* the storm came; he said *when* the storm came, the house fell. And you can trust me: the storms do come! But a house with a good foundation will withstand the storms, while those houses built on sand will crumble.

~ *Thoughts for Action* ~

- You are building your child's foundation.

- Laying the foundation is not glamorous work, *but it is necessary*!

- Without a solid foundation, the walls and roof will crumble.

- With a solid foundation, the structure will weather the storms!

Through skillful and godly Wisdom is a house (a life, a home, a family) built, and by understanding it is established [on a sound and good foundation]. And by knowledge shall its chambers [of every area] be filled with all precious and pleasant riches.

Proverbs 24:3 (Amplified)

Following a Blueprint

"It is better to build children than to repair men."
~Frederick Douglass

Let's settle it: You will not do a perfect job parenting! None of us will do a perfect job. There will be some repairing that needs to be done. But that is no reason not to go for the 10; we may end up with an 8 or a 9, but we should still aim high.

Our streets, schools, and prisons are full of young people and adults who need to be repaired. Someone did not count the cost, did not gain wisdom and understanding and knowledge of what the Master architect had in mind.

The enemy has battled for righteous seed from the beginning of time. He is battling like never before for this generation. He has tried to infiltrate our homes, our schools, and our churches.

John 10:10 says the enemy comes to kill, steal, and destroy. As he works to distract, to disarm, and dumb-down to a "new normal," he is attempting to destroy our young people and our families.

We need to guard that we don't allow the world's view to become our picture of what is the "normal family." Humanism has its agenda, and it is quite sophisticated. There is a fashioning through our culture that has an agenda of darkness. The enemy starts grooming our children, especially through media, from the time they are little, so they/we are accustomed to living out dark principles and not even realizing they are contrary to the Kingdom of God—contrary to who we have been created to be.

The product: the arrows we are assigned to fashion straight and strong are coming out splintered, bent, and weak. Many young people don't even know there are created as arrows, to be launched into the future as difference-makers. They have lost their way! In fact, many families have lost their way.

Your family has a heritage. And it will stand for something. What will that be?

You are making history. There is no other job that is impacting for eternity like yours. It is a job that will last for a lifetime. Actually, beyond your lifetime—and it will affect history. Your children will one day say, "I came from the _____ family." What will that mean?

Today, the family has taken a back seat to media, pop culture, and peers. Technology, which was intended to improve our lifestyle, has come in to divide and conqueror us. We need to ask ourselves, "Have we become a media-centered family or a relationship-centered family?"

Who what has the greatest influence over your children? Who are you giving the minutes of your children to each day? You are given the gift of 1400 irreplaceable minutes every day—how will you spend those? Will you invest those to make a difference in your children, your family, and your future? Twenty years from now, what will be stored in them?

There are a lot of pulls. Peer pulls. Activity pulls. Job pulls. Making more rules, buying more things, giving more privileges or being "cooler" is not the answer. Our children need our time and influence. The time you invest now will NEVER stop paying back. Sometimes with as busy as we are we can appease guilt by vying for our children's favor. We compromise our job of training to "have a good relationship." We might compromise discipline and training to "enjoy the time we have together."

As a parent, you must remember that your number one goal is not to build a relationship. A relationship with your children is immensely important, but trying to build a relationship first is like fashioning the rooms of a house and neglecting to lay the foundation. And then, parents wonder why the "house" is unstable—shifting and collapsing. When the storms come, the foundation is not firmly in place.

I see parents whose hearts are so precious and whose desires are so right, and yet they find themselves feeling like they are not getting the results they envisioned. In fact, they are getting results that are opposite of what they envisioned!

As parents, we desire to do a good job; we desire to have a happy, blessed, harmonious home. But often, parents find themselves stuck doing nothing more than "trying to keep the peace." They have to negotiate with their children, enduring temper tantrums and moodiness. They chase after their children and repeat themselves continually, struggling to keep a peaceable home. These parents work so hard to 'be fair and understanding'— to build a relationship with their children—and the outcome is not what they envisioned.

One can often be tempted to cater, coddle, give in, comply, and compromise in order to achieve the "picture of a harmonious and happy home." And often, the end result is frustration. Instead of the results these parents expected, their children become rude, unmannerly, demanding, self-centered, challenging, and difficult to handle. So the parent tries harder to win approval—to build a relationship—and thus the cycle has started. Out of frustration, these parents eventually make unfair demands of their children—especially once their children grow older. And so, peer relationships become much more comforting and fun to their children. This disappointing cycle perpetuates itself, and it often seems impossible to alter, as everyone works to cope.

When I was going to Bible School, I learned a great lesson on how true this is. I drove a school bus for a short season. And let's just say, I definitely gained some wisdom through life's experiences…

At the bus barn, they urged me to be strict—to lay down the rules and be tough at first. They told me I could become friends with the students later.

My first two loads were high school students. I needed no extra encouragement to comply with the advice they had given at the bus barn! There were so many of them when they filled the bus, and they were so big they swallowed up the aisle. All I could see in the rearview mirror was a sea of teenagers. I knew that if there was any chance of this going well, I had to dominate and rule. Because most of them were larger than me, the first decision I made was to stay seated at all times.

At the bus barn, they had also told me that I would be held responsible for the upkeep of the bus and for any expenses incurred from damage to the bus. One day after I started this glorious job, a seat was cut with a knife. From that day on, I checked all the seats before and after they loaded and unloaded. I started telling the students that I knew right where each one of them sat (*as if I could remember where they all sat!*), and that they would be held responsible for any damage to the bus or any mess left behind them on the bus.

One day, my eye caught a wadded-up sheet of paper flying through the air—the boundaries were being tested.

"*Did she mean what she said?*" they were thinking. "*Will she follow through?*"

We were on a country road, at a Stop sign. In my big mirror, I eyed the section the paper had come from.

"Pick up the paper," I said.

No movement.

I repeated it, this time more firmly. "I said, pick up the paper."

Nothing.

"I am not a trash collector and this in not a trash can. Pick up the paper."

No movement.

"We are not moving until you pick up the paper."

"But we're in the middle of the road," one of them said. "You can't stop here."

"I am stopping here until the paper is picked up. This is the last time I am saying it. PICK UP THE PAPER."

By this point, I was praying really hard under my breath. "Lord, what am I going to do if they don't pick up the paper? HELP!"

Just then, a boy moved from his seat and retrieved the wadded paper. I thanked him, and we continued on the route. (I think the kids were happy they didn't have to find out what I was going to do next…but they probably didn't realize that I was happy for the exact same reason!)

I never had another piece of trash thrown on that route—not even a gum wrapper left on the floor. There was never any more damage done to the seats. I had established authority and boundaries. The rest of the semester, that route was fun. The kids and I had a great time together—relationships grew and developed, and it was pleasant to see them every day.

On the other hand, I did not heed the counsel from the bus company for the darling kindergartners and first graders. They were not scary or intimidating. They were cute, huggable, sweet. They were so small! From the first day, I worked on establishing a relationship with them—you know, being fun and friendly and reaching out to them. I never bothered to establish boundaries or authority! There was no need for all that, right?

Um, right?

Yeah…

The procedure in leaving the school was that one bus after the other would leave the school, sort of in a follow-the-leader style. I had to get my children settled down so I would be ready to leave when it was our time to go. At first, I would raise my voice and tell them to sit down. Soon, they no longer listened to that. My next strategy—I would bang my keys on the metal ceiling to get their attention. Soon, that no longer worked either. My children became dull of hearing! Next, I resorted to pumping the brakes. It wasn't long before the other buses started leaving me behind.

Eventually, I began to roll forward and pump the brakes as I went. One day, as I was rolling away from the curb and pumping the brakes—the bus rocking and jerking under my command—a boy jumped up in the aisle with his arms outstretched, and he shouted, "Hold on, everybody! She's at it again, she's at it again!" Clearly, I had NO control.

The grand finale was so unreal, I still barely believe it myself! On the last day of school, as I unloaded a group, a boy grabbed a hose from children who were playing in the front yard…and he squirted me, right inside the bus!

On one bus, I established authority first and then moved into relationship. On the other, I went for relationship where there was no foundation of authority; because of this, I could not dominate.

Later, I was so grateful for that experience. It rocked the way I understood authority and boundaries. It impacted the way I worked with children of all ages and the way I raised my own. (Isn't it special how God takes messes and uses them to teach us so much!)

When my children were teenagers, they were one of the greatest joys in my life. They gave me pleasure beyond what I could have imagined—certainly beyond what people had told me to expect from teenagers.

But one of things I did was, when my children were little, I never focused on gaining their friendship and approval. I focused on building the foundation.

I never aimed to be on "the favorite" list or to be told I was "the best mother in the world." Every mother wants to hear those things—and of course, I wanted to hear those things myself—but my primary concern was that I would someday stand before God and hear *Him* say, "Well done, thou good and faithful servant. You fashioned arrows fit for the Master's good use."

Too often, parents try to build a relationship during the season that should be set aside for foundation-laying.

But as a parent, you need to ask yourself this question: **What is my goal?**

Is your goal to be your child's best friend? To be their buddy? Or is your goal to build children who are arrows fit for the Master's good use?

You do not need to be overbearing, harsh, and unapproachable. Far from it! In fact, once you have established your boundaries, there is so much freedom for fun and relationship. Once you are clear of who you are and what your job is, there will be no need to stand behind some false façade that says, "I'm the boss, be afraid of me." Once you establish your word as your bond, and clearly establish your vision, it is easy to relax and be in a relationship with your children at every stage of their growing and adult years. And in this way, you *will* be on "the favorite" list. They *will* tell you that you are the best mother. They will be your buddy.

But your focus is the job God has given you: Build a strong and solid foundation upon which they can build a life that will stand the storms of life.

~ *Thoughts for Action* ~

- Your number one goal as a parent is not to build a relationship; your number one goal is to lay a solid foundation.

- As you lay a solid foundation, the relationship will follow!

For we are fellow workmen, laborers together, with and for God; you are God's garden and vineyard and field under cultivation, you are God's building.

According to the grace of God bestowed on me, like a skillful architect and master builder I laid the foundation… but let each man be careful how he builds upon it.

For no other foundation can anyone lay than that which is already laid, which is Jesus Christ.

I Corinthians 3:9-11

Three-Part Beings

*You are a spirit; you have a soul,
and you live in a body.*

Children are asking us: "Who am I?"

You might think, "All I hear them asking for is juice!"

Well, they are asking for that too; but they are also asking who they are, even though they might not know how to express this question.

One of the most important aspects of training our children is teaching them **who they really are.**

And even though every child is different, the answer to the question "Who am I?" is the same for every child. In fact, it is the same for every single person!

Who are we? We are a three-part being: we are a spirit, we have a soul, and we live in a body.

It is important for you to recognize this, and for you to enable your children to recognize this as well. Even though your body is the part you see, it is not "the real you." Your body is merely your "earth suit," through which you contact the natural world. When our body stops working, the real "us" leaves this earth.

Your spirit, on the other hand, is the real you—the part that is created in God's image.

John 4:23 says that God is a Spirit (a spiritual Being), and Gen 1:26 tells us that God said, Let Us (Father, Son, and Holy Spirit) make mankind in Our image, after Our likeness, and let them have complete authority over the fish of the sea, the birds of the air, the beasts, and over all of the earth, and over everything that creeps upon the earth.

The spirit has a voice. The body has a voice. And the soul—the mind—must make a choice as to which voice it will listen to. We call the soul the "chooser." If the soul chooses to side with the spirit, the body will follow. If the soul chooses to follow the impulses of the body, the spirit will be dragged into it.

With our spirit, we contact God—for God is a Spirit.

With our body, we contact this sense realm—this world—and the Bible says that Satan is the god of this world.

In order for your children to not be ignorant of Satan's devices, you must share with them this foundational principle: <u>We are a spirit, we have a soul, and we live in a body.</u>

When you demonstrate this to your children—showing them how the spirit wants to pull them one way, the body wants to pull them the other, and the soul (their "chooser") must decide—you will be shocked by how readily they grasp this. In fact, I have never worked with a child who did not immediately "get it" when this revelation was shown to them. The reason children get it is because it is truth—it makes sense of life!

It is amazing how children as young as two years old can understand the world of the spirit, how it operates and how they fit into it. When children are told the truth about the choices they must make—to either listen to the voice of their spirit or to the voice of their flesh—it enables them to divide and separate who is talking, and it gives them the ability and power to make a choice. The earlier you practice this with your children, the greater freedom your children will experience.

This is the most important Kingdom principle to teach children. It empowers them with the authority that Jesus gave them—to rule and dominate.

We cripple our children when we continue to rule over and boss their bodies. If we always boss their bodies for them, they have to assume no responsibility for their choices, and they will continue to be ruled by their senses. After all, the world our children are most in contact with is the physical world, and if they are never trained to make the right decisions on their own—to boss their own body—they will naturally choose to follow the flesh. The first place a child can learn to walk in their God-given authority is over their own flesh. If they are trained to make choices based on choosing the voice of their spirit, they will be able to make the right choices for their own selves later in life.

Even children who are not raised in a Christian home are able to grasp this concept—the idea that bad choices are pulling them one way and good choices are pulling them the other, and they must always choose.

II Corinthians 4:16 & 18 tells us that there is an inward man and an outward man. We must learn to separate the two, training ourselves to hear and discern the voice of each.

It is our job to show our children where the conflict lies—helping them understand what is going on inside them. We must show them that **they** are not **their actions**! It is not:

- "I'm a bad boy."
- "My mother is mad at me."
- "I am dumb in school."
- "I get in trouble all the time."

None of this is the truth! The real **them** is their spirit—created in the image and likeness of God. And the problem lies with choosing the wrong side of the conflict—siding with the flesh.

The greatest gift we can give our children is the ability to choose spirit over flesh—without our help! Naturally speaking, there are certain things our children will do developmentally. However, when all we rely on is the "natural development" of our children, we fall so short of what God wants for us. We must develop the spiritual understanding of our children, helping them grow in sensitivity so that we can achieve results far superior to "the natural norm."

It is imperative that you train your children to listen to the voice of their spirit. This is such a healthy concept for them (for all of us), because it enables us to have a perspective of the struggle within ourselves. It also separates the lies that try to damage their self-esteem by labeling them as "bad," "loser," or "trouble-maker." No—it is just a matter of understanding they have been choosing to go with the voice of their flesh.

We all have made wrong choices. But if we understand the struggle that goes on within us, we will be able to equip ourselves to make right choices. What we feed grows. If we feed on what the flesh likes, the flesh will prosper. If we sow to our spirit and make sure we are feeding our spirit with God's Word and an environment conducive to spiritual growth, our spirit will grow stronger and will dominate.

Rather than surrounding ourselves with elements that pull on our senses and make it easier to gravitate toward our flesh, we need to feed on spiritual things and surround ourselves with the Word of God. In this way, we will become much better equipped to make the right choices—choices that side with our spirit!

~ Thoughts for Action ~

- You are a spirit. You live in a body. And you have a soul (a mind) that must constantly choose between the two!

- You *cripple your children* when you boss their bodies for them!

- If you boss your children's bodies for them, they become unable to choose right over wrong without your help.

- The greatest gift you can give your children is the ability to choose right over wrong—the ability to side with their spirit—*without your help*!

- Make it easier for your children to listen to their spirit (instead of their flesh) by surrounding them with things that feed their spirit (instead of their flesh!).

For those who are according to the flesh and are controlled by its unholy desires set their minds on and pursue those things which do gratify the flesh, but those who are according to the Spirit and are controlled by the desires of the Spirit set their minds on and seek those things which gratify the Spirit.

Romans 8:5

Equipping our Children with Knowledge

In order to raise children who make right choices, you need to equip them with knowledge!

Have you ever arrived late to a movie? Your mind works like crazy to figure out what is going on—who is good, who is bad, what is the story? Sometimes it takes us a while to sort it all out.

Sometimes, we get tricked into thinking the bad guy is good, and vice versa.

The journey of life can be similar. Here we are, dropped into God's Story—in the middle of this timeline—and it may take us a while to figure out who is good and who is bad (and by this, I do not mean your neighbors or family!). In time, we learn that GOD IS GOOD; we have an enemy who is a poser, and there is a story going on all around us. But this story is not just any story…

There is a war going on!

This war is between the kingdom of Light and the kingdom of darkness. We happen to be part of this war! I am part of it; you are part of it; our children are part of it. In fact, everyone is part of it—just not everyone knows it!

Yes, whether we want to acknowledge it or not, there is a war going on. As Christian parents, we need to equip our children for battle. It empowers our children when we tell them who the enemy is and what his intentions are. We need to tell them what our enemy looks like, what he wears, how he "dresses," what he says, and what weapons he uses. If we do not give our children this information, how can we expect them to recognize him?

If we simply tell our children that something is "wrong" or "bad," but fail to give them the full picture, we are not really equipping them. We are just giving them rules—but not empowering them. There is a difference between saying, "Don't hit your brother" and saying, "If you are hearing in your head to disobey your mom and hit your brother, whose voice is that talking to you?"

Ask your children, "Do you know why the devil wants you to obey him? He wants to be your boss, so you will think you are happy, and you won't be learning how to choose to listen to your spirit and obey God and get *allllllll* the fun and wonderful blessings He has stored up for you!" "His job (the enemy) is to trick you and teach you how to listen and obey every idea he puts in your head." "He's jealous and doesn't want you to have God's best."

This is quite a difference. One is just plain rules. The other empowers your children to understand the devil's strategies so they can walk in authority over these strategies—even as a young person!

I Peter 5:8 tells us that the enemy is seeking whom he MAY devour.

For toddlers and young children, I often use a dilapidated puppet and provide little examples for them, so they can get a picture of what their enemy acts like. The puppet will whisper in their ear, "Disobey your mother; hit your brother; take that toy; no one will know." After all, they hear these things every day, don't they? They just do not hear them audibly.

When these kinds of thoughts pop into their head after they have seen this example, a child will realize, "That's the enemy talking." I have even heard children say, "No, Devil. Get out of here in the name of Jesus! I am not going to obey you or listen to you."

I have had parents express concern that it will scare their child to know there is a battle of good and evil, and that there is a devil. I have NEVER seen that happen. Even the most gentle child perceives a sense of empowerment. Their inner world falls into place and makes sense with this knowledge. Now they can identify what they have already been dealing with. It is like an adult who has an AHHA moment. They get it.

For our teenagers, media is a strong vehicle that entangles them in a web—one that feeds them, satisfies them…and depletes them of what will really strengthen them and equip them for spiritual success.

What are we, as parents, doing to counteract this? Are we simply telling them what they "should not" or "cannot" do? Or are we giving them a picture of the entrapments of the enemy?

Why should our children refrain from sex before marriage?

Why should our children avoid looking at pornography?

Show them the blessings God opens up to those who follow His "highest and best," and show them the entanglements, bondage, and loss of freedom that result from not following His "highest and best." Explain these things to your children—even when they are young: a moment of pleasure lures you in, and it leaves you with lasting pain, baggage, and regret.

Withstand him; be firm in the faith…
I Peter 5:9

Look carefully then how you walk! Live purposefully and worthily and accurately, not as the unwise and witless, but as wise (sensible, intelligent people),
Making the very most of the time because the days are evil.
Therefore do not be vague and thoughtless and foolish, but understanding and firmly grasping what the will of the Lord is.
Ephesians 5:15-17

You do not want your children to be causalities of ignorance. Equip them! Make your children battle smart! Teach them more than the "WHAT's; teach them the "WHY"s—the vision of why we do what we do.

> *...I have set before you life and death, the blessing and the curses; therefore choose life, that you and your descendants may live.*
>
> Deuteronomy 30:19

When I taught Kindergarten in a Christian school, I taught the children these principles. They became proficient in determining when a classmate was choosing to listen to their spirit or their flesh.

Often I would hear, "Mrs. Tohline, so and so is choosing to listen to their flesh!" Sometimes I would even hear, "Mrs. Tohline, so and so made a right choice and listened to the voice of their spirit." They were acutely aware of the power of choice. And that's what I was looking for.

Your spirit has a voice. Your flesh has a voice. One leads to blessings. One leads to temporary pleasure, sin, and trouble. As a parent, it is our job to help our children discern between the two voices and understand the war going on inside them. You can see why we started this book with understanding our role as a parent: we, too, need to walk in these truths of choosing to listen to our spirit and choosing NOT to listen to our flesh!

> *He who heeds correction and instruction is not only himself in the way of life, but is also a way of life for others. And he who neglects or refuses reproof not only himself goes stray (but also) causes to err and is a path toward ruin for others.*
>
> Proverbs 10:17

And Colossians 3:2 tells us to set our mind, and to keep it set on the things that are above—on the things of the spirit.

Who sets the mind?

Who keeps it set?

We do! Wherever the mind is set, that is the side that will "win." It is that old "two against one" concept. If the mind agrees with the body, the spirit will be dragged along in the bad choice. If the mind chooses to go with the spirit, the body will have to be quiet and comply. Sometimes, the voice of the body is so loud, it becomes difficult to choose…

As our children grow in understanding, we must sometimes help them choose.

OUR PURPOSE AS PARENTS IS TO…

- HAVE CHILDREN WHO ARE LED BY THEIR SPIRITS.

    Why?

    - SO WE WILL HAVE TEENS WHO ARE LED BY THEIR SPIRITS.

        Why?

        - SO WE WILL HAVE ADULTS WHO ARE LED BY THEIR SPIRITS!

You don't just wake up one day and know how to be led by your spirit. You don't wake up one day and just start listening to your spirit! It takes training. It takes conditioning.

The Bible says that children left to themselves will be ruled by their senses, and will bring their parents to shame.

Your goal should be to train your children to make an impact on their world. As we train our children, we do so with destiny in mind.

When children catch a vision of destiny and purpose, their ultimate goal will not be to drive or drink or "get away from home" and do as they please. When they catch a vision of destiny, they will instead desire to find their course, run their course, and finish their course with joy. In this way, they can avoid the 'teenage/college-age' warp that so often diverts children from purpose, impact, effectiveness, and destiny.

One of the greatest gifts we can give our children is an understanding of the importance of destiny.

Destiny is precious; and it must be protected. We cannot be casual in our approach to protecting destiny. We cannot be fearful. We must be intentional and focused on training our children to be able to follow their spirit.

~ Thoughts for Action ~

- Tell your children who the enemy is. Show them what the enemy's goals are.

- Show your children the war between their spirit and their flesh.

- Do not allow your children to be casualties of ignorance!

My people are destroyed for lack of knowledge....
Hosea 4:6

Training Our Children

*We don't tell our children what to do;
we train them to make right choices!*

Train: verb—*to point in an exact direction, mold the character, instruct by exercise, drill, <u>make obedient to orders</u>, bring into a position to grow in a particular way. To prepare for a contest—as the coach prepares an athlete.*

It is our job to train our children *to grow in a particular way.* Jesus is the way, and we are to train our children to follow Him. There is nothing within the definition of **Train** that implies "optional," "passivity," or "nonchalance."

Think of a good trainer shaping and training a prize horse. They do not wound or harm the horse. They do, however, bring the horse under submission so that the treasures, gifts, and strengths inside that horse can emerge. This implies a steady, active, and accurate leadership role.

As parents, we do not carry a passive role; it is definite and exacting!

The Bible tells us in Proverbs 22:6 to train up a child in the way he should go.

To "train up" means to create a thirst within them. Remember, they are watching and learning. When you live your life "close to the cross," the light in your eyes rejoices their hearts.

When one of my girls was three years old, she said, "Mommy, you were the mommy I was hoping for when I was in your tummy." It was precious when she said it (it's still precious, when I think of it!), but it is also true that most three-year-olds feel this way. When a child is three, their mommy and daddy are the center of their world. Because of this, it is important who we are during that time, as it is during this time that our children are making sense of their world. You show your children "how life is done" through every part of your everyday living. They will take with them the things they see from you, and as they grow older and their horizons broaden, you can be that "iron that sharpens iron" for your children.

The second part of Proverbs 22:6 (after it tells you to train up your child in the way he should go) goes on to say *in according to his individual bent, so that when he is old he will not depart.* God has placed within our children His gifts and callings. Our job is to train them in His way, so that they will follow Him, and in following Him they will find their course, run their course, and finish their course with joy!

Our job is not to be heavy-handed with our children, *telling* them what to do and *controlling* their choices of sports activities, schools, careers, and spouses. Our job is to train them to hear and follow the voice of God. As our children grow, and we lessen our "control" over them, it will not be nearly as *scary* when we have trained them to follow their spirit, where God is leading them.

Isaiah 30:21 tells us that they will hear the voice of the Lord behind them saying, "This is the way—walk ye in it."

As we follow God's plan for training and launching our children, they will learn to hear and follow the voice of God. In this way, they will move from external control (with us, as parents, helping them make the right choices) to internal control, where they hear the Lord behind them saying, "This is the way—walk ye in it."

This is the ultimate goal—for each of our children to be able to police their own flesh. This takes training; and remember, training is different from "telling" or "scolding"!

In I Samuel 1:11, it tells us that Hannah did not doubt Samuel would serve the Lord, because she had trained him to fulfill his purpose.

But Eli's sons were disobedient and immoral, and in I Samuel 2:23-25 we are told that Eli scolded his sons, and "they harkened not to their father's voice."

I Samuel 3 tells the story of Samuel hearing the Lord's voice. He had been trained to have an ear to hear, and he had also learned to listen and obey!

Training is required in any aspect of life where a particular result is desired. We are trained to drive a car, be a fireman, and teach school. Any job you think of requires training to succeed! And the training we are doing as parents will matter for eternity.

If we want our children to succeed in life, it is up to us to train them, helping them learn to listen to their spirit rather than to their flesh, and helping them to understand that there is a purpose in their life that is bigger than them! Spirit-led children are those who have submitted their wills, learned to live outside of themselves, and come to understand there is a purpose for their life that is bigger than them.

∽ *Thoughts for Action* ∽

- You are training your children to make right choices—to listen to their spirit instead of to their flesh…

- …and as you do this, you are steadily transferring the responsibility to them! You are preparing them to *move into their own life* with the knowledge, understanding, and ability to make right choices!

Train up a child in the way he should go [and in keeping with his individual gift or bent], and when he is old he will not depart from it.

Proverbs 22:6

Choices

*The greatest gift you can give your children
is the ability to make right choices!*

C hristianity is not a place of restraint, but of Choice. We all make choices every day. Some good. Some not.

*...I have set before you life and death, the blessing
and the curses; therefore CHOOSE life...*

Deuteronomy 30:19

As a parent, you serve as the identifier for your children; it is up to you to know which choices are of the spirit and which are of the flesh. It is up to you to help your children CHOOSE life!

*The thief comes only in order to steal and kill and destroy.
I (Jesus) came that they may have and enjoy life, and have it
in abundance (to the full, till it overflows).*

John 10:10

When my children were young, I reminded them all the time that their spirit and body each had a voice, and they would have to choose which one to listen to. The spirit wanted to obey God, and the flesh wanted to…eat all the cookies in the cookie jar! As we mentioned already: *You don't just wake up one day and know how to be led by your spirit. You don't wake up one day and just start listening to your spirit! It takes training and conditioning.*

And it is important that you realize this: Children *can* learn! In fact, it can be *easy* for them to learn to "boss their body."

Here is a great dialogue example that I adapted from a post my daughter did for my blog – she uses this in her classroom. It works anywhere!

"When you use self control, you are telling your body what to do and making it listen to you. When you do that, you get all kinds of privileges, because Mom can trust you to make the right choices all by yourself. But if you don't choose to make the right choices on your own, you are choosing Mom control.

"You are saying to me, 'Mom, I can't make my body listen to me by myself, I need your help.' Mom control is not fun, because I'm not going to follow you around to make your body do the right thing. When you choose Mom control, you are choosing consequences. You are choosing to lose the privileges that you earn by being responsible."

Consistently enforce this, and it will become clear to them. When they break a rule or do something that isn't acceptable, don't get angry; there is no scene, no reason to take it on you. It was their choice, so put the responsibility right back on them.

Oops! Wrong Choice

"Oh no! That was a wrong choice you made, wasn't it? You know what happens when you make wrong choices…You get consequences every time. I'm so sorry that you made that choice. I'll bet next time you're going to make the right one."

No drama…You don't have to get frazzled and upset. It wasn't your choice. It was their choice.

This way of thinking is so liberating, not just for us but for them as well. They begin to feel empowered.

"It's not because mom is mad. It's because you made a wrong choice. That means next time you have the power to change your outcome."

Obviously, they still get emotional and angry when they are receiving their consequence. But, use this as another opportunity to reinforce the power of their choice.

"I can see you are so upset right now. Are you upset with me, or with your choices?"

Ninety-nine times out of a hundred, the answer, through tears, will be, "My Choices!" But even when the answer is, "YOU!" it's the perfect opportunity to calmly redirect their attention back to their ability to choose.

"I didn't make the choice to disobey. You made that choice, and I feel so sad for you. I'm sure next time you're going to remember this and choose differently."

These are some key phrases I used when my kids were little, to help them make right choices:

- You be the boss of your body.
- Are you **choosing** to listen to your flesh or to your spirit?
- Did Jesus tell you to say that (or do that)?
- What **choice** are you going to make? Are you going to **choose** to listen to your flesh or your spirit?

Our job is twofold: Firstly, our job is to help our children recognize the voice of the spirit and the voice of the flesh; Secondly, Our job is to help them choose.

It is important that you use the word **CHOICE**. Because, truly, the choice is up to them! This is the case when they are young. It will continue to be the case as they grow older. And it will especially be the case when they move out on their own! And the sooner they understand that they are *choosing*, and that every *choice* has a consequence, the easier and more victorious their lives will become.

Don't many of us wish we had this help ourselves, learning this as children? So many teens, young adults, and even mature adults never take responsibility for the *choices* they make.

Children left to themselves will be ruled by their senses. It is up to us to help them understand what is going on inside them. When our children can discern between the three parts of their being, every choice becomes simpler.

Galatians 5:16-25 lists the works of the flesh and the fruits of the spirit.

These are some of the works of the flesh: selfish, stingy, critical, fearful, lustful (a strong desire toward something more than God) anger, vengeance, negative, complaining, lazy, confused, lacking peace, overindulgent, not wanting to get involved.

And these are the fruits of the spirit: love, joy, peace, patience, kindness, goodness, faithfulness, gentleness, and self-control.

When children "break rules," they are actually "checking boundaries." Instead of saying, "Why did you do that, you know better than that!" say to them, "I see you made a wrong choice and listened to the voice of your flesh when you chose to_____."

"I bet your spirit was talking to you and saying, 'Don't do it, don't do it.' Right? Well, that silly flesh—we have to discipline it so it will obey you and let you listen to your spirit. My job is to help you by correcting the flesh when it bosses you around. So let's go and get a correction and show that flesh who is boss, right? I think you are going to boss that flesh the next time it tells you what to do, right?"

When your children begin to understand the war that goes on within them, they will actually tell you when they have listened to their flesh! They will no longer see it as "getting caught," but rather, they will see it as bringing their flesh under control in order to hear their spirit—the part of them that is in communion with God!

When your children hear you say to them, "Listen to your spirit," or, "You made a good choice—you listened to your spirit," it affirms within them the power of choice and the process of making the choice to listen to their spirit. Sometimes, they will choose spirit, and other times they will choose flesh. If they make a wrong choice, do not scold them; instead, say to them, "Oops—you **chose** to listen to your flesh. And that was not a good **choice**. My job is to help you **choose** to listen to your spirit so you will be able to hear and follow God all the days of your life."

After this, the consequences can follow; in this way, your children will understand that you are helping them "boss their body." After all, this is the job given to you by God—to train your children to hear and obey their spirit and learn to follow God.

～ Thoughts for Action ～

- Christianity is not a place of restraint; it is a place of CHOICE.
- Your job as a parent is twofold:
- Firstly, you are supposed to train your children to recognize the voice of the spirit and the voice of the flesh.
- Secondly, you are supposed to help them CHOOSE!
- The sooner your children understand that they are choosing, and that every choice has a consequence (negative consequences for wrong choices and *positive*

consequences for right choices), the easier and more victorious their lives will become!

- Your job as a parent is to train your children to *hear and obey* their spirit and *learn to follow God*.

…I have set before you life and death, the blessing and the curses; therefore CHOOSE life, that you and your descendants may live.

Deuteronomy 30:19

The Value of Words

*We are all training every day,
whether we know it or not,
whether consciously or unconsciously.*

Every day, we are training with our words! When you speak to your children, watch your patterns; after all, your children are watching them also! They know when you *mean* what you say (even if you do not). They know how many times you will say something before they need to pay attention. They know what tone of voice means, "Okay, *now* I really mean it!" Your children know when you will repeat yourself, when you will yell, and when they had better take action.

When you tell your child, "Put on your shoes; it's time to leave the house," what does that mean to them? Does it mean nothing, because they know you will say it three more times (and on that fourth time—you know, when you start *yelling*—you finally mean it!)? Or do they know that they have until you start counting down—"I mean it: Ten…nine…eight…seven!"—before they have to pay attention?

Do they know that if they fail to obey, you will (gasp!) march upstairs and put the shoes on their feet yourself?

Or when you say, "Put your shoes on; it's time to leave the house," do you truly mean what you say?

Our children are Master Boundary Checkers. Every day, they check the boundaries to see how secure they really are. They search for any "holes" in the fence, for any "gaps" in the rules. And as the parent, you have to stay on your game, because they are constantly pushing and testing. You might have to remind yourself at times of who is in charge and who is leading this crew!

The number one way God communicates with us is through (that's right!) *His Word*. God created the world using words. Jesus healed the sick using words. The entire Kingdom of God is built on words and the value they have.

Furthermore, God's *Word* is how we get to know Him. And if our children come to a place where they do not see words as valuable—as having authority—they will not grow into the understanding that God's Word has value and authority!

The integrity of words is lost today—and this is no accident! A man's word use to be his bond. It would be common to hear, "He gave me his word." What was behind his word was all he and his family's name represented. But words have lost that power today. The enemy has diminished the value of words so that God's Word—written on a page—holds no value in the eyes of many.

Training our children to trust in and understand the value of words sets the foundation for them to trust in and understand the Word of God.

Can your words be trusted? In our families, we often put "words" in a position where they hold very little weight. Children start out believing words have power—this is a natural state of mind—but then, there are those times when you say something to your child and they receive it as a promise…only for this promise to go unfulfilled. "But you *saaaaaaid*!" And when your child tells you this, they are usually right—you *did* say! And you diminish the power of words when you do not follow through.

The same goes for those times when you say something like, "Put your shoes on; it's time to leave the house." Children soon learn that words are really not that important if your words, as the parent, have no power. "If you do that one more time, I am going to…" And the child does it again, and you repeat the same threat! "Don't do it again. If you do, I am going to…"

Where's the power? Exactly!

We are the first example of 'God' our children see—the pattern they believe God to be like—and it is imperative that we place the same value on our own words that God places on His!

Beyond the areas of "instructions," "corrections," and "promises," it is also important that you realize how important words are in shaping a child's view of their own self.

Just as we look to God's Word to see a reflection of how He sees us, our children are looking into the mirror of our words to see how they look. Your children are canvases. Every day, you are picking up the brush and painting the picture that forms who they believe they are.

Words are like a container that delivers something; they can carry life-giving words or death-producing words.

Words are alive. They *live*. Words are tangible and they affect the realm of the Spirit. We feel their effect. Jesus said, "My Words that I speak to you are Spirit and Life." They carry something. Jesus said His Words carried Life. We have all experienced words that carried death.

I still remember negative words that were spoken over me by a teacher; I still remember something negative said about me by another adult I trusted. Those things stick in a child's head; they stand out—even more than the positive things stand out.

That saying, "Sticks and stones may break my bones, but words will never hurt me" is not true at all. Words *can* hurt, and they do. Words *can* injure—and if you are not careful with your words, you can injure your child.

> *Death and life are in the power of the tongue, and they who indulge in it shall eat the fruit of it [for death or life].*
> Proverbs 18:20

Are we not all inspired when someone speaks words of greatness to us—something that gives us a larger picture of us than we see of ourselves? Think of your words as seeds that will one day reap a harvest. And consider the sort of harvest you will reap off the words you are choosing to speak.

∽ *Thoughts for Action* ∽

- God painted the world using his Words.

- Your children are canvases, and with the words you speak to them each day, you will be painting their worlds. You will be painting the way they see themselves. You will be painting their futures.

- You will be painting the picture of who your children believe themselves to be.

- Words are meant for life, but they can also be used for death.

- Your words are not rods; they are not meant to be used for scolding your child. Use your words to train your child.

- Always let your words mean what they say, so that the value and authority of your own words will reflect the value and authority of the Word of God!

A man's (moral) self shall be filled with the fruit of his mouth; and with the consequence of his words he must be satisfied [whether good or evil].

Proverbs 18:20

Listening and Obeying

*When we have ears to hear,
we access the blessings of God!*

God's Word lists so many blessings that are available to those who choose to listen and obey. And as the stewards of our children, it is our job to train them to have "ears to hear."

If we allow our children's hearing to become "dull" and "calloused," we cripple them from being able to hear and follow God.

God is not in the business of repeating, yelling, scolding, or begging—and we should not be either! Instead, God has given us the ability to CHOOSE, and He has given us the tools to make the right choices. And of course, this is the same thing we are supposed to do for our children, lest they end up in a place where they fit these words:

...you have become dull in your spiritual hearing and sluggish even slothful in achieving spiritual insight.

Hebrews 5:11

The world tries to lock us into our senses, and to desensitize us spiritually. We soon become hardened, calloused, petrified, and paralyzed toward the things of God's Kingdom. God desires for us to practice our listening skills. His Word is full of promises He wants to give us if we will listen and obey. The promises are based on the ability to hear and obey.

As parents, our purpose is to develop within our children a consciousness of God. And the earlier you begin, the easier it will be!

The first step is this: you must train your children to be sensitive to *your* voice—to hear and obey. As you train their ears to hear—to follow and obey—so they will hear and obey the voice of God.

In order to achieve this, you must watch over the words you speak; and make sure you are speaking excellent and princely things. This is a great responsibility! And in order to fulfill this responsibility, you must exercise self-control, learning to keep your tongue. After all, if you are going to mean what you say, you better make sure you are saying the right things!

One day, when our older daughter was about four years old, she kept interrupting me on the phone. And my husband said to her, "If you interrupt your mother when she is on the phone again today, you are not going to the church party."

My daughter interrupted me again. There was a problem, however: We were the pastors. And we were giving the party at a friend's house. And since everyone in the church was going, there would not be anyone to babysit!

Oops…

So, what did we do? Did my husband change the punishment to something different? Did we sit down with our daughter and have a talk instead?

Nope! My husband stayed home from the party also, so that he could keep his word to our daughter. You would think, *Well she is only four, what does it matter?* Did we say, "Oh well—there will be another time when we can make the point that we mean what we say"? It was tempting! But to this day, she says she remembers that—she says that event stood out to her for years as proof that Dad meant what he said.

Of course, we got smarter after that and made sure we came up with consequences that did not impact us as well! But on that day, my husband stuck with what he said—because we knew how important it was to convey to our daughter the importance of words. She knew she could take what we said as truth!

When we realize the power and the weight of our words we will weigh them and choose them more wisely. We need to mean what we say—and we need to see that this is not at all about us! It is about the job we have been given, to launch the children God has entrusted to us.

Our words are tools. When you realize this, you will think through the process of your words instead of telling your children (over and over again!) to do something until it is finally "time to start yelling."

When you say "No," does it mean "No"? Or does you child know they can change your mind if they start whining, crying, pouting, or begging?

One day, my youngest daughter had some friends over. They asked me if I would take them somewhere, and as I thought it over, one of the girls clasped her hands in front of her: "Oh, *pleeeeease*, Mrs. Tohline—pretty *pleeeeease!*" My daughter just stared at her. As the girl kept it up, my daughter said, "Don't do that—that means nothing to my mom."

Of course, this does not mean that your children are not allowed to discuss things with you! For instance, if I told my children, "Thirty minutes until we are leaving the house; make sure your stuff is cleaned up in thirty minutes," and one of my children came to me and said, "Mom, I have a game set up in the living room—may I leave it there until we get back?" (and if there were no guests coming over when we returned—no specific reason why it had to be cleaned up right away), then I would tell them, "Of course!" It is important that you do not become a dictator, where *What Mamma says goes*, with no explanation as to why! No one likes living under a dictator, but on the other hand, it is very difficult to respect a leader with no direction or ability to lead definitively.

You need to train your children to communicate their thoughts with words, as opposed to throwing a fit when they don't "get it their way." When they throw that fit and it "works," you have just trained them that they have negotiating power when they "throw a fit." When they get their desired outcome, you are actually rewarding the flesh and causing more work for yourself, as well as dulling them spiritually.

Successful communication should start early—after all, you will be training your children to communicate in life.

～ *Thoughts for Action* ～

- Is your lack of follow-through with your words causing your children to be dull and calloused to the value of words?

- Does your "Yes" mean "Yes," and does your "No" mean "No"?

- Can your children change your mind by begging, pleading, or whining?

- Are you training your children to communicate? I used to say, "Talk to me with your happy voice," when they were screaming, whining, or crying to express themselves.

"I'm a wise child. I make my mom and dad's heart glad. I listen to Wisdom. Wisdom is my friend."

This was a saying we used A LOT in our home, taken from a few Proverbs that I strung together. I made up a little tune for this and used it when our crew was having an "opportunity" to make a right choice.

Training Their Ears to Hear

Our job is not to tell our children what to do. Our job is to train our children to make the right decisions!

When you give instructions to your children, make sure you have their attention. After all, it is no good to say to your children, "I *told* you that [fill-in-the-blank]," and for them to say, "I never heard you."

With my children, if I called to them, I expected them to confirm that they were listening.

"Yes, Mom."

"Five minutes until we will be leaving."

"Okay, Mom."

And if they did not respond, I would model what I expected of them. If I called them and there was no response, I would say, "Yes, Mom."

"Yes, Mom," they would say.

When training your children, always model the acceptable response.

If I asked them to do something they did not want to do, I might say, "That's okay, I'll obey."

If my children slipped into that whiny voice, I would say, "I'm a winner, not a whiner."

If I gave my children instructions and they were interrupting or were not focused, I might say, "I am teachable, Mom. I can hear and obey."

In this way I modeled what I expected instead of just getting frustrated. That is *training them in the way they should go.* They don't know the way—that is our job!

I used to play "listening and obeying" games with my children. One such game was the "Stop Game." When they were little, I would say, "Go," and we would run. Then I would say, "Stop!" And we would freeze immediately.

One day, after shopping as a family, we were in the parking lot, and my three-year-old son started galloping ahead of us between two cars. My husband and I could see what our son could not: a car was coming up the next lane. My husband and I both said, "Stop." He stopped on a dime! It was simply normal for him to listen and obey on the first try. But on that day, it was extremely important!

Another game we played to work on listening skills was "One, Two, Three." I gave my children three verbal instructions that they were supposed to follow in order, and I could not repeat what I had said. For instance, "Run to the refrigerator, clap your hands three times, and say, 'I am happy, happy, happy!'" As they got a little older, they would ask for more instructions. "Give me four now." "Give me *five!*" We were having fun, but I was also "training their ears to listen."

In parenting with destiny in mind (with the BIG PICTURE in mind), we must train our children to walk in the promises of God. And part of this is training our children to hear His voice. Let's look at just a few of the 'rewards' for having ears to hear:

> *Oh that they might have a heart and mind in them to keep my commandments …that is might go well with them and their children forever.*
>
> Deuteronomy 5:29

> *Obey the voice of the Lord…and then it will be well with you…*
>
> Jeremiah 38:20

> *If you are willing and obedient you shall eat the good of the land.*
>
> Isaiah 1:19

> *If you obey My voice…you shall be my own treasure.*
>
> Exodus 19:5

> *Children obey your parents in the Lord [as His representatives], for this is just and right. Honor your father and mother—this a the first commandment with a promise-*

-that all may be well with you and that you may live long on the earth..

Ephesians 6:1-3

This sensitivity to God's voice doesn't *just happen* one day. It is developed little by little. The first steps of being able to "hear and obey God's voice" is training our children to be sensitive to our words. I would often say to them, "Listen to my voice". Or, "I am training you to hear and obey my voice so that you can hear and obey God's voice, so it will be well with you". When children begin to listen to the little things in their spirit, they will be set to hear the big things later in life!

And your ears will hear a word behind you saying, This is the way; walk in it, when you turn to the right hand and when you turn to the left.

Isaiah 30:21

When my older daughter was seven, we were on a family excursion to Toys R Us. Each of my children had some Christmas money to spend. My husband was with my son in the boys' section, looking for the right gift for him. I was with my daughters, looking at things girls like to see. My older daughter wanted to go to Daddy while I continued shopping with her sister. (In those days, we felt safe for her to travel from one parent to the next in the store!) Later that evening, she told us what had happened on her way to her dad.

As she went looking for my husband and my son, she approached the stuffed animal aisle. She already knew she did not want another stuffed animal to add to the huge menagerie we had, but she started walking toward that aisle anyway. Then, she heard in her spirit, "Don't go and look; you will be tempted to buy one, and that is not what you want." She told us later that she put her head down and kept walking all the way to Dad. What a victory for her! And that opportunity to exercise 'listening and obeying' to her spirit prepared her to listen later, as decisions became bigger.

Remember this: As parents, our job is not to tell our children what to do. Our job is to train our children to make the right decisions! It is your responsibility to move your children toward self control.

Parenting is not about exerting external control. It is about training internal control! As long as it is about us—the parent, controlling externally—our children need to take no personal responsibility for their own actions.

Personal Responsibility does not happen all at once—it is a process. When we begin our journey of parenting, we take on 100% of the responsibility. Our baby is helpless—they are dependent upon us. But as our baby grows daily, they gain strength, ability, sufficiency, and might. Every day, our children move constantly toward independence, and with greater independence comes greater opportunity to choose.

Exercise your child's "self-control" muscles when they are young, and they will be strong in these areas as they grow older!

If you keep a bit in your child's mouth and try to control their actions and attitudes, you will not empower them with the tools they need to succeed in life. If you do not train your children to take responsibility step by step, there will come a time when their independence grows larger than their self-control—and this results in trouble.

> *I the Lord will instruct you and teach you in the way you should go; I will counsel you with My eye upon you. Be not like the horse or the mule, which lack understanding, which must have their mouths held firm with bit and bridle, or else they will not come with you.*
>
> Psalms 32: 8-9

This scripture is the heart of why we are doing what we are doing—training our children to be sensitive to their spirit. It's like running a marathon: You don't decide today that you are going to run a marathon this next weekend. But if you train regularly with the marathon in mind, you will be able to accomplish this goal!

Internal control is the same way. You must build and develop your children, gradually shifting responsibility their way. This is so important! After all, we all know what happens when a parent sends a child who has no internal control off to college (where there is no external control!).

If our children are going to develop into adults who can take responsibility, it will come from understanding—not from rules. Rules are good—in fact, rules are necessary! But too many rules is nothing but a lot of external control.

My husband was big on making sure we did not have a lot of rules in our home. All the time, he said, "The rule in this house is listen and obey, so you can hear God and listen and obey His voice." As your children come to *understand* who they are, what their enemy looks like, and what the privileges are that are attached to their destiny, they will be able to discern this voice and follow it!

If we have too many rules, on the other hand, our children will not have to take personal responsibility. And if they do not *have to* take responsibility, chances are they will not.

We cannot stress this enough: Do not make all the decisions for your children! Not even for a two-year-old. Always direct them to choose. "What is your spirit saying to you?"

The flesh always wants what it cannot have. If you tell your children they cannot have something, they will push and push, and it will become your responsibility to keep them controlled. You want your children to boss themselves. Let *them* set some boundaries; hand over some responsibility.

My son collected baseball and football cards when he was in elementary school. At his birthday parties, he often received these prized cards. Whenever he received important cards in plastic sleeves, he would get so excited! One time, he turned to me: "Oh, Mom—can I please open them?" It took me so off guard, because I knew how strict he was about the conditions of his cards. After I recovered from the shock of his question, I said to him, "Sure you can, if you want to." Once I said this, he had to move from *wanting* external control to *exercising* internal control. "Well," he said, "maybe I shouldn't." I told him I thought this was a good idea. The peer pressure that day had caused him to look for external restraint. When our children "ask for permission" for what they already know is wrong, they are wanting to give you responsibility for their actions. If it becomes your responsibility to restrain them, they can choose to listen to their flesh.

It is so important that we realize (and that we convey to our children!) the fact that we do not follow an "I can't" Gospel. Rather, we have discovered who we are, what we have been given, and the amazing destiny attached to our life. Therefore, we choose not to do certain things, because they are only counterfeits to all God has for us as His children.

Our purpose in parenting is to train spirit-led children who are sensitive to the leading of God.

Our goal is not good children. Good children are pleasing to people. They know how to behave. They might 'get through life without being contaminated by the world.' Good children are well-taught. But they are not the ultimate goal in parenting.

Our goal is to have spirit-led children who understand the purpose in their life. We want to equip our children to affect the world, to be the salt of the Earth that makes a difference, to be the voice that is heard, and to be an influence that brings change to the places they go.

Parenting is not "defensive"—protecting your children from the big bad world.

Parenting is offensive—training your children to go out and change the world!

~ Thoughts for Action ~

- If you want to train your children to walk in the promises of God, you need to *train them to hear His voice.*

- Train your children to hear the little things now, so they will be prepared to hear the big things later.

- Your job as a parent is not to tell your children what to do; your job is to train them to make the right decisions.

- Parenting is not about exerting external control; it is about *training internal control.*

- If your children are going to develop into adults who can take responsibility, it will come from understanding—not from rules!

- Are you trying to raise "good children" who follow rules, or are you striving to raise spirit-led children who make a difference in the world?

If you will listen diligently to the voice of the Lord your God…all these blessings shall come upon you and overtake you…

Deuteronomy 28:1-2

BOUNDARIES AND DISCIPLINE

Discipline

*The road to life
is a disciplined life.*

Some of you might have skipped previous chapters and jumped straight to the chapter on discipline. "This is the chapter I need!" you might be thinking. But there is a reason why we have saved this chapter until now: You will not get the results you desire if you do not build toward discipline using the previous chapters. If you have skipped any earlier chapters, go back! Without the foundation laid by those chapters, you will not achieve the desired result when it comes to discipline.

What is the desired result of discipline?

> *Moreover, we have had earthly fathers who disciplined us and we yielded to them and respected them for training us. Shall we not much more cheerfully submit to the Father of spirits and so truly live? For our earthly fathers disciplined us for only a short period of time and chastised us as seemed proper and good to them; but He disciplines us for our certain*

good, that we may become sharers in His own holiness. For the time being no discipline brings joy, but seem grievous and painful, but afterwards it yields a **peaceable fruit of righteousness** *to those who have been trained by it – a harvest of fruit which consists in righteousness- in conformity to God's will in purpose, thought and action, resulting in right living and right standing with God.*

Hebrews 12:9-11

The desired result of discipline is to bring forth peaceable fruits of righteousness!

The secret behind every champion basketball team, magnificent orchestra, or successful business is the principle ingredient of discipline. Therefore, it is a great mistake to require nothing of children and to place no demands on their behavior. Self-control is not produced in an environment that puts no obligation on the children.

Discipline has received a bad rap because of misuse due to a lack of understanding. Because of this, many precious parents who dearly love their children wouldn't think to spank them. They instead use words and psychology to do the best job they can. Additionally, there are those who have struck their children out of frustration or anger, causing harm to the body—and worse, to the emotions.

Now, if you say spanking is not for you, these principles will still work—but you will still have to train the flesh with some action of discipline, apart from simply scolding! The Message Bible says it this way:

> *At the time, discipline isn't much fun. It always feels like it's going against the grain. Later, of course, it pays off handsomely, for it's the well-trained who find themselves mature in their relationship with God.*
>
> Hebrews 12:11 Message Bible

Remember what we have talked about already: Parenting all boils down to training your child to choose between their flesh and their spirit! If they do not grasp the concept of the consequences that come from listening to their flesh, they will have a hard time learning to consistently make the right choice!

The Bible promises many things to those who bring their flesh under control. Proverbs 10:17 tells us that the road to *life* is a disciplined life. Proverbs 15:32 says that an undisciplined, self-willed life is puny, but an obedient, God-willed life is spacious!

When it is presented like this, it makes the choice pretty easy. After all, I know I would vote for the spacious life! And I have seen this lived out in children who are God-willed; they are living their dreams, doing more than they imagined possible, and continually growing in a thriving fulfilling relationship with God.

∽ *Thoughts for Action* ∽

- Discipline is: Training that molds, corrects, and perfects.

- Discipline is: To bring under control.

- We discipline our children to bring them under control, and we train them so they gain self-control (an ability to bring their own self under control!).

- A team does not "just happen" to win a championship; a player does not "just happen" to become a championship player. It takes discipline. The coach is not trying to be a "nice guy." A good coach molds, corrects, and perfects the team—bringing them under control!

- If you want to be "liked" by your children, discipline them! When they become champions in life, you are the one they will thank.

A refusal to correct is a refusal to love; love your children by disciplining them.
Proverbs 13:24 (Message Translation)

What Godly Discipline is Not

Your child's job is not to "keep you happy."
Your child's job is to listen to their spirit!

I read an article in *PARADE Magazine* that suggested the way to stop violence in America is to stop spanking children. The article stated that parental spanking promotes the thesis that violence against others is acceptable, saying that spanking is the first half-inch on the yardstick of violence. Spanking, the article said, is followed by hitting, and ultimately by rape, murders, and assassination. It stated that the model behavior that occurs at homes sets the stage of, 'I will resort to violence when I don't know what else to do.'

This is why it is so important to understand *how* to discipline your child! In addition to the fact that—if you are not regulating the media your child is ingesting—they are likely seeing violence all the time on television, in video games, and in movies (which certainly promotes violence as well!), it is absolutely true that a parent sends a message of violence when they discipline their child while mad, angry, or frustrated. Additionally, spanking your children when you are angry sends the following message to them: "WHEN I MAKE MOM OR DAD MAD, LOOK OUT—they are going to spank me." But that is not Biblical discipline! *Discipline is not supposed to be about you!* It is not about *you* being happy or mad. It is about your child having made the wrong choice. It is about training your child's flesh.

> *Discipline your son while there is hope, but do not indulge your angry resentments by undue chastisements and set yourself to his ruin.*
>
> Proverbs 19:18

If you are angry, you probably should have attended to the situation sooner. But now, it has gotten to a point where your flesh is riled up! Sometimes we get preoccupied, or busy, or LAZY, and we just don't want to "deal with it"....so we ignore it. If we simply desire "good" children, "better than most" children, we can overlook a lot of attitudes and behavior. But this is WRONG! It is our job to take care of these things—to discipline our children, to not ignore it when they are doing something that needs training. God has entrusted these children to us, in order for us *to mold the character and point them in an exact direction.* This is serious business we are talking about. It is our job to deal with their flesh—to train them until they are able to make the choice to boss their own flesh and use internal control.

Godly discipline is not using words as rods of discipline.

Many of us need to read that more than once.

Godly discipline is not using words as rods of discipline! We should never use words that berate, or that paint a picture of something God Himself does not paint for your children in His Word. Remember: Words have power! When dealing with your children, you need to use your words to paint the picture of "Life."

Furthermore, discipline is not nagging or scolding—nagging and scolding will only make everyone tired, and will destroy relationships. Corrections with words will not train the flesh. Corrections with words are instead applied to the soul, and these words continually create the image of someone God did not create them to be. This becomes an extremely negative cycle for the child and the parent.

It is not your children's job to *keep you happy*. This is not fear-based, anger-based, approval-based, or performance-based relationship. Our children must be under loving command, and not tyrannical command. Parenting is not a power trip! You need to see your role as a mentor and a leader, submitted to God and the job He has given you to do. And the job He has given you to do is to love your children while training them to be arrows for Him—training them to listen to their spirit, and not to their flesh.

When we feel angry or hostile toward our children, it is the result of our own disobedience to the Lord's command. Your child's job—and your job, as well—is to be pleasing and obedient to God. You must also make choices to walk in the spirit and not fulfill the dictates of *your* flesh.

∽ *Thoughts for Action* ∽

Things on the "Never Say" list:

- "Bad boy/girl."
- "You make me so mad."
- "I am so angry with you."
- "Why did you do that to me?"
- "You have made me so mad, I have to give you a spanking/time-out."

On the "Okay To Say" list:

- "You made a wrong choice."
- "You chose to listen to your flesh."
- "I guess you were checking to see if the boundaries were still in place."
- "You chose to listen to your flesh, and it is my job to correct your flesh. But that is okay, because we are training you to listen to and obey your spirit instead of your flesh, right?"

What Godly Discipline is Not

Fathers, do not irritate and provoke your children to anger (do not exasperate them to resentment), but rear them tenderly in the training and discipline and the counsel and the admonition of the Lord.

Ephesians 6:4

Discipline Keys

Set boundaries;
They create a secure environment!

It is important to know the developmental stages of your children. Children do things because they are progressing in their development. We do not discipline for childish behavior that is a part of developmental stages! However, we need to be careful that we do not excuse behavior that should be molded or corrected—behavior that is just the flesh 'checking out the boundaries' of what is acceptable and what is not.

This is so important to realize; it is such an important part of raising your children. You need to know the difference between rebellion and development—between those things that require discipline and those things that do not. For instance: A child spilling milk or forgetting their jacket or having an accident are not things to scold or discipline! This might seem obvious—a piece of cake!—but things get more complicated than this.

Developmental charts will help us understand what is childish and what is rebellion. There are a lot of resources available to understand your child's developmental stages—and every parent should have these on hand.

Establishing Rules

Rules need to be enforced. Because of this, it is wise to have simple rules—ones you can keep track of and follow through on. As I mentioned already, the main rule in our home was: LISTEN AND OBEY MY VOICE.

Why? Were we dictators?

Absolutely not! (And neither are you!) But we needed to be sure our words possessed power.

The bottom line of parenting is this: You are training your children to hear and obey God's voice.

Here is a dismal picture portrayed of sons who were "taught and informed" but not "trained":

> *He (Eli) said (after hearing all his sons did), Why do you do such things? For I hear of your evil dealings from all the people. No, my sons; it is no good report which I hear the Lord's people spreading abroad.*
> *…Those who Honor Me I will honor, those who despise Me shall be lightly esteemed.*
> I Samuel 2:23-24, 30

I know I have mentioned this scripture in Isaiah before. But, really look at what it says—it is powerful.

And your ears will hear a word behind you saying, This is the way; walk in it, when you turn to the right hand and when you turn to the left

Isaiah 30:21

Isn't that what we want? Children who can hear and follow God? And your children will not learn to hear and obey the voice of God (who they cannot see!) if they cannot hear and obey the voice of their parents (who they can see!).

Children can have selective hearing—they can choose when and what they hear. If they don't "hear" you, then they don't need to obey you. Therefore, I always required a response, such as: "Yes, Mommy," or "Okay, Mom," when I was talking to them.

Once you establish your rules, discuss them with your children. There is nothing wrong with "regrouping" when you feel like you have gotten off course. Have a 'family meeting' and let everyone know the adjustments that need to be made. *Be a team*—get input from the children, finding out what they think is working and what they think is not working.

Your children don't make the rules—but input from those on the team is appreciated, is in fact valuable, because the team needs to feel like they have a voice and can be heard. After you receive input, you can make decisions. It is up to you to know where to take the team, to know what adjustments must be made.

Post the rules where they can be seen; make sure they are understood, and make sure the consequences are understood also! Remember: You must remain consistent! Whatever you set as the rules in your household must be enforced. If your children feel a rule should be changed, listen to them while they explain their point of view. (And no, I'm not talking about the negotiating that wants to take place just before discipline is administered!) Until a rule has been changed, it must be followed!

Maybe you have small children, and one rule (that they know good and well!) is "No jumping on the bed." If you see them jumping on the bed—or see evidence they were jumping on the bed—you must correct them, because these precious gifts from God (these young arrows you are meant to shape) are testing the boundaries, trying to find out if the rules are real.

Are your rules real? Do you tell your children, "Next time you jump on the bed, you are going to get a correction?" If your children know the rules, and they do not follow the rules, you must do your part to train them. I know it is inconvenient to stop and discipline for every little thing. It is muuuuuuuuuch easier to overlook and "pretend" you didn't notice. Again, if this was about "good children," you'd be fine. But you must keep in mind your own obedience to the Lord's command to train up your children according to Isaiah 28:10, precept upon precept, line upon line, and here a little and there a little.

Jumping on the bed might seem like such a small thing—*Oh, they were just having fun, I'll let it slide*—but as your children grow older and check the boundaries, the stakes become higher.

Don't wait until the problems grow; take action now!

One mistake many parents make, when they know their child has done something wrong (but the child does not yet know that the parent knows), is to ask their child, "Did you do [fill-in-the-blank]?" When you do this, you open the door for your child to choose to side with the flesh again—to add lying to the list of infractions. Don't ask your children if they did something (giving them a chance to lie); don't ask your children why they did something (giving them a chance to make excuses or try to pass the blame!). Tell your children they made a wrong choice—that they chose to side with the flesh—and remind them what the punishment is for disobedience.

Do your part!

Too many parents equate permissiveness with love. Permissiveness is not love; it might feel better at the moment, but in the long run, you are setting your children up for failure!

When a child hits a boundary, one of two things will break: The boundary, or their flesh. If your boundaries are flexible—if your children know they can get away with certain things with you, even though you told them those things were outside the boundaries—you will reinforce their tendency to choose to listen to the flesh. It might not be a 'big deal' today. In fact, today you can feel like a pretty great parent. The trouble is, the path of their future you are laying for them is not one of success…it might sound harsh, but it is more likely a path of heartaches and failures.

When you were in school, did you ever have a teacher who could not keep control of the class? If you experienced this, you know you ended up not respecting that teacher—no one respected that teacher (sort of like me with the kindergarteners and first graders on the school bus!). You might have felt sorry for them, but while in school, you did not respect them.

Keep that in mind: Permissiveness does not show love! *Godly authority shows love.*

When your goal is to be friends with your child—to have your child 'like you'—you will end up compromising what is good for them, and will probably also fail in getting your child to really like or respect you! That's a lose-lose situation. But when you train your child to hear and obey God's voice—conditioning them by training them to hear and obey your voice—your children will respect you, and friendship will be a byproduct of this relationship.

Love grows out of respect!

And it all comes down to training your children to hear and obey your voice—*so that they can grow to hear and obey the voice of God!*

They Do It Because They Can!

Recently, I did the thing I try to avoid at all costs: I went to the grocery store on a Saturday. We had been out of town for two weeks and needed food badly, so I really had no choice—but I at least thought that getting in there early would be smart. Apparently, quite a few moms with children had thought this also. Really, the store was fairly empty—except for the moms with their crews in tow.

When I shop, I am usually in my own world, with my list in my face. I like to get in and get out as quickly as possible. But on this day, I became aware of my surroundings at the milk case. A mom had a girl in her cart, and a big boy who rode on the front of the cart.

I watched for a bit as he helped his mom. As he carried a milk jug back to the cart, she said to him, "Don't drop it." When he got to the cart, he lifted the gallon jug above his head and proceeded to thrust it into the cart. The jug flew by the little girl and hit the cart with a wallop. I gasped out loud. The mom, already tense, gathered her boy back onto the cart and continued down the aisle.

I felt stressed, and as I rounded another corner I came across a mom with three children, two of whom were crying over snacks in the cereal aisle. Now, I was no longer paying attention to my grocery list. I was hearing. There were cries of children all over the store.

They are winning, I thought. The children are winning! The moms are just trying to get in and out of the store with the least amount of stress possible. But the children are winning!

Then this phrase popped into my mind: **They do it because they can**.

Back when our children were little, it was no different. Children are always testing boundaries. And they know when they have you in a compromising place. We have all seen it—They act out, because they know they can get away with it.

I hope I do not sound as though children are evil—plotting their revenge and uprising against parents while waiting for the next opportunity to be defiant.

No—children are simply doing what they have been created to do: strive toward independence. And along that journey, they are always testing the boundaries to see where they are secure and where they are weak. The grocery store is a major playing ground in this battle of who's the leader! Public places, they seem to know, are where the boundaries weaken.

Settle it. Know it. Set your game plan in place.

I would have "the talk" if I felt like the children needed reminding before we embarked on a journey. The talk did not include bribes—"if you are good then we will…" I was not going to bargain for good behavior. The *expectation* was good behavior, and the consequences for choosing differently were clearly defined. There were only a few times I had to leave the store, go to the car, discipline my child, and return to what we were doing.

It was a lot of effort—especially in the winter when all jackets had to be put on to return to the car. However, my boundaries became believable because my word was with power.

It does take effort, absolutely. But is it worth it. Without a doubt! The stress I felt that Saturday at the grocery store for all those precious moms just reminded me—it is soooo worth it.

Don't be duped into thinking that kind of behavior is normal and acceptable. You don't have to feel like taking your children into public is like playing Russian roulette and just hoping you have a successful outing. Of course there will be challenging times, and unexpected situations—but I want to encourage you to build a different expectation and platform of raising your children. They can behave well. They can learn the process of choice and self control. They can learn to make right choices and choose which voice on the inside of them they will obey.

Keep your expectation higher than what you see every day. When we are looking for different results, we need different expectations!

∽ *Thoughts for Action* ∽

- Your children will not learn to hear and obey the voice of God (who they cannot see) if they cannot hear and obey the voice of their parents (who they can see!).

- Are your rules real? Or do your children know that they can get away with shifting boundaries?

- Remember: As your children grow older and check the boundaries, the stakes become higher!

- Permissiveness does not show love.

- Authority shows love!

- *Love grows out of respect.*

Correct your son, and he will give you rest; yes, he will give delight to your heart. Where there is no vision [no redemptive revelation of God], the people perish; but he who keeps the law [of God, which includes that of man], blessed is he.

Proverbs 29:17-18

Respect

*You must show respect to your children
in order for them to show in respect to you.*

Respect is so important. Not just for your children to respect you, however—but also, for you to respect your children.

"Okay," you might say, "but what does respect look like?"

The key to treating your children with respect is to ask yourself this: "How would I want to be treated?"

This does not mean spoiling your child, indulging them, catering to their appetites of the flesh. (After all, would we really want to be treated this way ourselves? In the long run, the answer is no!) What this *does* mean is treating your children with respect and dignity—remembering that they are special gifts, and treating them in accordance with this realization.

I cringe in the grocery store when I hear a parent speak rudely to their child. Just the other day, I saw a mother turn around and say to an 8- or 9-year-old girl, "I am so sick and tired of you talking!" Wow! The little girl's face sank. She was crushed **and** embarrassed.

Now, that girl probably WAS annoying her mother. But Mamma reacted instead of walking in a leadership role.

I don't know the situation, but many options come to my mind:

- "Honey, Mom has to concentrate right now; please hold that story until I get this done."

- "There is nothing more to discuss about this situation right now. If you want to talk about it some more, we can do so after dinner."

- "I have already given you my answer. To keep asking will result in the loss of [a particular privilege]."

When we, as parents, are disrespectful to our children, we need to look inside and see what is triggering our reaction. Often, there is something unpleasant working in our emotions and our children become the scapegoat for our venting. They are easy targets. But check your heart and ask yourself why you are reacting as you are. If there is pressure—and you have identified that it is coming from the children—address the behavior as the leader you are. If there is another issue, just identifying it will help you to not transfer it to your innocent children.

Another area to check concerning respect is how we are managing their behavior. Have you seen children who are self-willed? They are obedient and respectful as long as things are going their way. But if you analyze the situation, you will realize that the children are leading. They have trained their parents/grandparent to do as the child wants so all will be well. The parent has learned how to keep the peace by using bargaining power and making deals in order to move through their day.

"If you are good, you will get a treat when we are done."

I'd rather have this approach. "When we are done, we are going to have a treat." My expectation is my children will behave, show respect, and listen to their spirit. If they choose not to, then the expected discipline will follow. The behavior is separate from the next activity.

If you do like the approach of a reward for respectful and obedient behavior, then you must make the boundaries very clear and definite and not something you are going to hold over them as your leverage of control. Always ask yourself, "Is this picture of a person who is really leading and training?"

Granted, children know when you are the most vulnerable—usually when we are distracted or preoccupied. Remember, they are the Master Boundary Checkers. This can lead to us "giving in" and changing the boundaries "just this one time." Don't be deceived! There is no better time than NOW to enforce the boundaries and remain the leader.

~ *Thoughts for Action* ~

- Show your children respect by: Never putting them in a situation where they feel uncomfortable, afraid, or powerless.

- Show your children respect by: Never embarrassing them.

- Show your children respect by: Disciplining your children with respect, dignity, and love when they need to be corrected.

- Show your children respect by: Using your words to uplift them (and never using your words to degrade!).

- Show your children respect by: Working to make life a win-win situation.

Boundaries: Setting Guidelines for Your Family

*The purpose of correction
is to train your children to listen to their spirit.*

Obedience is not automatic. It is learned. For some children—those who are more compliant—obedience comes more easily. At the same time, however, we have all seen the compliant child who is 'standing up on the outside, but sitting down on the inside'—a child who is outwardly obedient, but not from the heart. Whether there is outward disobedience or inward rebellion, both are of the flesh and need to be corrected so your children can grow in the way God intends.

This is all about the battle of the will—the child's own battle between flesh and spirit. This is where we come in. Our job as the parent is to help them not only make the right choice, but make it for the right reason!

> *Correct your son, and he will give you rest; yes, he will give delight to your heart.*
>
> Proverb 29:17

When you encounter behavior in your home about which you are unsure whether it is wrong or right, ask yourself: "Does this behavior bring rest and delight?" Don't make a reactive decision, according to how you feel on that particular day, but make your decision based on what makes your home the place you want it to be. And this evolves as your family matures.

Sometimes, you will set boundaries based on what gives you rest and delight, rather than based on whether something is necessarily "wrong" or "right." For instance: In our home, jumping on the bed was not allowed. For one thing, I saw it as unnecessary, and as being a poor steward of what we owned. But for another thing, it did not give me rest and delight! The same went for screaming or loud talking in the car. In the car, we used our inside voices—because that gave me rest and delight. These were not reactive decisions; these were boundaries! I knew where the boundaries were. My children knew where the boundaries were.

I let my children keep multiple toys out at once. Sometimes their toys were all over the place. I felt this allowed them to use their imagination, to create, to have fun! Twice per day—at noon and at the end of the day—we would clean up everything that was out. These were the boundaries in place.

Did it ever bother me when their toys were all over the place? Of course it did! There were days when the clutter overwhelmed me. And sometimes, I would tell my children this: "Sweetie, Mommy needs you to make sure you clean up your toys as you go along today. Tomorrow, you can have lots of toys out at once like normal, but today, let's try to keep just a few toys out at once." But my children would never 'get in trouble' for the clutter—because there were no boundaries set against it! The main thing is that the boundaries are not set up as reactionary rules. That does not show respect. If you are having "one of those days" and you need different boundaries for that day, explain this in a respectful style—as a great leader—and they will feel respected, and can respect you. There is such a difference between leading with respect and "flying off at the handle."

Maybe you allow your children to jump on the bed, but you absolutely cannot stand when toys are all over the place. If this is the case, set these boundaries! And as you expect your children to stick to the boundaries, you must stick to them as well.

Proverbs 29:18 says that where there is no vision (no redemptive revelation of God), the people perish; but he who keeps the law of God is blessed, happy, fortunate, and enviable. This scripture is used a lot, but notice that it follows verse 17—which talks about correcting our children! If we do not have the vision of why we are doing what we are doing, we will not be effective.

In 2 Corinthians 10:12 it says, "...when they measure themselves among themselves and compare themselves with one another, they are without understanding and behave unwisely." We need to be sure we are not measuring ourselves among ourselves—in other words, what is our measuring line? Where do we get our boundaries from? Don't base what you do on what another family does. That does not create stability or respect. Those parents are not the gatekeeper of your family. What is okay for one family may not be for another. When our children were in high school, we would often hear what was "okay" for the pastor's children to do. We'd smile, because Mama Pastor said she heard that a lot...I'm sure lots of children were pulling "that card." The great thing was, it was none of our concern what they did—stricter or more lenient than us. We were called to be the gatekeepers of our family, and we were not measuring ourselves by what others did or didn't do. Therefore, we were not grabbing for control as our children got older, nor were there random rules popping up out of fear. As the gatekeeper, you will give over more and more control to your children, so they can guard their own gates. As we did this, we always said, "We still hold the reins. We let them out and we can pull them back in. We let out more and more slack as long as we see you are behaving responsibly and guarding your own gate. If we need to pull the reins back in, we will until you can have good oversight yourself."

Decide—for your family—what brings rest and delight.

~ *Thoughts for Action* ~

- Even if your children have done something others might not see as "wrong" (leaving toys out, jumping on the bed, etc.), they are still in disobedience if these are tests of the boundaries you have set. When your children test the boundaries, do not fall for the excuses.
  - "Oh, I forgot."
  - "Oops, I won't do it again."
  - "I didn't know you meant *this* bed."
  - "[So-and-so] told me to do it."
  - "[So-and-so] did it."

- You are not in the business of negotiating and giving credence to excuses. You are in the business of training your children to assume responsibility for their choices!

- You are the Gatekeeper. You hold the reigns and determine how much oversight of their temple your children can assume.

However, when they measure themselves with themselves and compare themselves with one another, they are without understand and behave unwisely.
I Corinthians 10:12

Disrespect and Challenging Authority

*Children will check boundaries,
making sure they are still in place!*

Disrespect:

How can you tell the difference between a child who is frustrated and attempting to express himself and a child who is challenging authority and exhibiting disrespect?

The attitude is usually a clear indication. Is he being hurtful, defiant, deceptive, manipulating? These are signs of disrespect and challenging authority. A child who is frustrated and a child who is doing his best to express himself might look similar at first glance, as he lashes out because of his inability to put word to his feelings.

Getting down on eye level and helping him express what he is feeling will take him a long way in walking in respect.

On the other hand, disrespect will only grow if you let those seeds sit in the ground. Hurtful words, condescending attitudes, and abusive actions are disrespectful and should not be tolerated. At whatever age children exhibit disrespect, it should be dealt with! Disrespectful attitudes, actions, and words are all of the flesh—and if they get away with being disrespectful with you, they will also be disrespectful to others.

When a child is disrespectful, don't take it personally. How you react matters. If you "get hurt," you have ceased leading. If you get angry and lash out, you are also showing disrespectful behavior.

It is hard sometimes to keep your cool, but you must! Remember: Leaders Lead. Keep in mind, they are challenging the boundaries. You are enforcing them.

Challenging authority:

When a child acts like they are on equal level with you, demanding and refusing to follow requests that are made, or when they have a smart mouth (to name just a few things), they are clearly challenging authority. Please do not make excuses for their behavior. You will not be doing yourself or them any favors.

When children challenge authority, it might feel like they are against you as the parent; but again, they are checking boundaries—just checking the fence to see if it is still in place. Don't take the lie that says, "I must not be a good parent if they are doing this." Realize that this is just their flesh, and you must help them correct this. It all part of the process!

If you have a rule in your house that says your children are supposed to come when you call them to come, and they tell you, "Oh, I didn't hear you," it is likely that they are checking boundaries. "I didn't hear you" is a classic excuse! After all, do you think they would have heard you if you said you were taking them out for ice cream? Probably!

You are training their ears to hear. Now (of course!), you need to make sure you know your children. Some children become engrossed in the things they are doing and genuinely do not hear. As my children grew up, it was required that they say, "Yes, Mom?" if I called them. This system worked for us, because I knew they had heard me call their name, and that they were now responsible for what I had told them. Come up with a system that works in your house so you do not deal with Selective Listening.

Remember: We are training our children to hear our voice so they can hear the voice of God!

The testing starts early—they want to know how secure the boundaries of your words are. The other day, my husband and I were coming out of the grocery store and a 3- or 4-year-old boy was walking with his grandma. She was pushing a full cart and she called him to hold onto her sweater. He kept running ahead toward the exit door until she said, "I mean it, you have to hold onto my sweater." He finally complied, and then—as they were walking—he once again let go and looked at her. My husband and I looked at each other and said at the same time, "He's testing the boundaries of Grandma."

Children also challenge authority when they "have a better idea that you" at every turn. This is a hard one. When we are training leaders, they often get ahead of themselves and "try to lead before their time!"

When I was teaching first grade, I had a little boy who was a strong leader. He could make a suggestion to the class, and they would jump to it and carry out his idea. Literally, I could have given instructions, only to be followed by an idea he verbalized, and—like a school of fish—they all turned and went with his suggestion! I realized that what I had on my hands was a strong leader in the making. But to be a good leader, one must learn to be a good follower.

One day I took this young man outside the class and asked him whose name was on the door. "Yours, Mrs. Tohline," he said.

"That's right," I told him. "My name is on the door, and your name is not here yet, is it?"

"No Mrs. Tohline, it isn't."

I proceeded to tell him that he was going to make a great leader someday, but he was not being paid to run the class; I was! So I was going to train him to be a great leader, by learning to be a good follower. This young man was not being rebellious or defiant; he just needed some help in using his God-given talent.

If a child is a gifted leader, they must be trained to come under authority. That is God's way. Many potential leaders never reach their destinies because the qualities were not properly directed and they were not trained. It is really all about attitude. When rules are broken, that is pretty concrete. What do we do with areas not as clearly defined? They can slip through the cracks since there is more "interpretation" involved. Let's look at some of those.

Rebellion

> *He who resists and sets himself up against the authorities resists what God has appointed and arranged in Divine order. And those who resist will bring down judgment upon themselves—receiving the penalty due them.*
>
> Romans 13:2

Rebellion is open resistance, a refusal to obey, or a resistance to authority.

We are told to resist the devil, but the devil has turned it around for us to resist authority! That's just what he did, and look what happened to him. Lucifer rebelled against God in Heaven. That was his downfall—his heart was hard and rebellious; he thought he knew more than God knew, and he and his followers were thrown out.

There is no good thing in rebellion…it is a sin, and it sets itself against the knowledge of God. When we put up with rebellion, we accommodate evil in our home. *Now* is the time to cut off the head of rebellion. Rebellion, which is the opposite of submission, has been at the root of man's nature since the beginning of time. When God gave Adam and Eve authority, it was under the submission to God. They rebelled, were outwitted, and ended up losing their God-given authority. We have been given back that authority through Christ Jesus when we live in submission to God's way of doing things. Of course, the enemy would like to outwit us like Adam, bring us back out from that authority, and lead us to live rebellious lives.

Children LOVE understanding that they have authority and knowing how it works. When you explain this to your children, you fore-arm them to resist the devil and the temptation to be rebellious. They can walk in submission and thereby in the authority and the blessings God has for them. This makes having authority over their flesh and the devil exciting and relevant.

If you are willing and obedient, you shall eat the good of the land; but if you refuse and rebel, you will be devoured by the sword. For the mouth of the Lord has spoken it.
Isaiah 1:19-20

And of course, if you have rebellion in you, you need to repent and submit yourself to God. Examine yourself. If you are not sure whether you have rebellion, ask God to show you! Rebellious attitudes need to be cut out of the heart and removed from your home.

Yes, rebellion is easier to identify in older children. However, if you stay on it when your children are little, you can stop it from gaining ground in your home. Tell your children when their behavior is rebellious. Let them know what the Bible says.

Keep in mind that there are times when your child will know more than you on a topic. But this does not mean that they have more wisdom, and this certainly does not mean that they have more authority! Knowledge does not determine rank and authority; God has delegated rank and authority to us, and we must follow God as we train our children to follow us.

The rebellious dwell in dry places!

Psalms 68:6

Strife

Servants of the Lord must not fight! Preserve the bond of peace.

From II Timothy 2:24

Preserving the bond of peace can be a tall order! When there is more than one person in a home, there will be more than one way in which something can be done—and this often leads to strife. Add children into the mix, and strife becomes a high probability!

In our home, fighting was not considered normal sibling behavior. We did not expect or accept as normal behavior that our children would fight with each other.

Often, I've heard parents say something like, "Oh they just fight like cats and dogs." "Oh, they are just acting like brother and sister and driving each other crazy." Did my children fight? Yes, they did. However, it was not acceptable. We did not embrace the philosophy of, "Oh, it's just what sibling do—they quarrel with each other." Nor did I think it was acceptable for them to get annoyed and treat a younger sibling without honor. I also did not expect a younger sibling to "intentionally annoy" an older sibling. Hateful words were not allowed. We did not even allow "shut up" to be said. Our rule was, "kindness is the rule for all I say and do." After all, the Bible says we must preserve the bond of peace and we must not fight.

Train your children to recognize that it takes two to fight, and train them to flee from strife! When two of my children squabbled with one another, they knew that they would both be corrected. I would remind them, "Where there is strife, there is confusion and every evil work." Strife is like opening the door and ushering the devil inside!

Strife is of the flesh. And realize: strife loves for someone else to assume the responsibility of control. When you mediate strife, you take the responsibility onto your shoulders. Don't you have enough on your shoulders already?

Don't take on the responsibility of your children's strife! This will only make your job more difficult—and it will keep your children from learning to police their own flesh.

Before you know it, you can end up with another role as the parent—mediating conflicts. ("But Mom, he said I was stupid!" "I did not! I said you were *dumb*. Mom, I didn't call him stupid, I promise!") And the more you mediate, the more the conflict seems to grow!

When it comes to strife in your home, use your judgment. Sometimes, you will have to step in—but try to avoid this as much as possible. Train your children to flee strife; and when they are caught in strife, teach them to resolve it. You will be happy that you are not stuck forever playing the role of "Squabble

Controller," and your children will be happy that they are learning to get along.

Train your children to realize that words are powerful. Hateful words are not acceptable. Name calling is not acceptable. Words are meant to uplift! When your children begin to flee from strife and to use their words for kindness, they will be rewarded in the long run with siblings who are not *just* siblings, but are best friends as well!

As our children have grown up, they have been each others' best friends. Yes, they got on each others' nerves, as any group of people living under the same roof do! But it has been truly amazing to witness how much respect and love they have shown to each other throughout all their years growing up. They now talk about how glad they are that they were raised to respect and enjoy each other.

You have to work to preserve the bond of peace.

Lying

Lying lips are extremely disgusting and hateful to the Lord, but they who deal faithfully are His delight.
Proverbs 12:22

Lying is...

Lying is defined as "a deliberate untruth," but *deceitfulness* (propagating beliefs that are not true, or not the whole truth) and *exaggeration* are also forms of lying.

Your children lying...

The characteristics of God are honesty and integrity. The word integrity is derived from 'integer,' which is a mathematical term. An integer is a whole number, as opposed to a fraction. When we walk in integrity, we walk in the whole truth—not a fraction of it. And if you want your children to walk in all the blessings of God—rather than in a fraction of the blessings—they need to walk in integrity (in 'whole truth'!).

Lying to your children...

So often, I see parents lying to (or being deceitful with!) their children, and I wonder if they realize that the seeds they are planting will yield a harvest—and it will be a harvest they probably do not want! Just as we have reminded ourselves over and over again throughout this book that we are to treat our children the way we would want to be treated, you should also realize that the way your children treat you will be a reflection of the way you have treated them. *What your children see, they will do.* And this goes for lies and deceit as well! Remember: You are the first picture of God your children see. Show them, by example, the honesty and integrity of God—the honesty and integrity you want them to walk in themselves!

Deceit is lying...

Deceit has some truth—but it is not whole. This is a real temptation for most of us. We must guard our hearts from deceit, as this one spreads easily! If I am running late for an appointment after I misplaced my keys, or after the traffic held me up, it is easy to blame those circumstances instead of truly owning my behavior. "Blame" is shifting the responsibility that I should own to someone or something else. We are not only being deceitful to others when we do this, but are also being deceitful to ourselves. As children grow, they need to see that who you present yourself to be is who you really are.

The Case of the Missing Gum…

I was helping in the 10-12-year-old age group at church when one of the teachers asked a young man to spit out his gum. She turned away as the boy walked to the trash can, but I watched while he leaned over the trash can and supposedly let the gum drop from his mouth! However, I noticed it did not drop from his mouth. Evidently, he has tucked it into his cheek.

Now, at first, I was upset. I wanted to "bust this kid"! But I asked God what I should do…

When the children broke up into groups for classes, I asked the young man to come with me to a private room. I had something special I wanted to share with him.

The boy was visibly nervous. I told him he had nothing to be nervous about—I just had something special I wanted to share.

Once we were in the room and he was sitting, I said, "God has His hand upon you…you know that, don't you? He has something very special He has called you to do."

The boy agreed. He said he did know this.

I continued. "Just as God has His hand on you, the enemy is always looking for an open door to get in and try to influence you. Today, when the teacher asked you to throw your gum away, God had me see that you did not throw it away. Do you know why He had me see this? It is not about the gum. The gum is just a small thing. But it is about the enemy looking for a door, so he can have influence. The enemy will suggest things, and if we choose to listen and follow these thoughts, this is the beginning of his influence—of him taking us down a path that leads us to one day wake up and say, 'How did I end up here?' It is not about 'not being caught,' either. You *did* get caught today. But not by me. You got caught when the enemy suggested, and you agreed. You got caught in his snare. God had me see this so I could expose the enemy to you—so I could show you, and so you will continue growing in wisdom." I reminded him that he had authority over the enemy—Jesus gave him this authority! I told him, "Don't get tricked into giving your authority over the devil by disobeying those who are in authority over you. Remember, it is not about being seen or not being seen by someone. The battle with the devil is in the unseen realm—and you have been given authority in that realm in Jesus' name."

I prayed with the boy, we hugged, he thanked me, and he went to class. Through this experience, I was able to impart strategies for kingdom living. It was bigger than, "I am the adult, and I said so. And here is your punishment!" He learned something that day—and he didn't just learn that he needed to figure out a better way to preserve his gum; he instead got a glimpse into the kingdom of God and its operations.

How our children *should* see it…

When my oldest daughter was in 5th grade, her teacher told the students that every one of them who remembered to bring a pencil to class the next day would be rewarded with a cookie. The next day, my daughter forgot her pencil! A friend sitting behind her offered her an extra pencil that she could claim as her own. My daughter declined. She told me later, "The devil can't buy me with a cookie!"

> *Food gained by deceit is sweet to a man, but afterward his mouth will be filled with gravel.*
>
> Proverbs 20:17

Complaining

> *And [when] the people complained, it displeased the LORD: and the LORD heard [it]; and his anger was kindled; and the fire of the LORD burnt among them, and consumed [them that were] in the uttermost parts of the camp.*
>
> Numbers 11:1 KJV

Complaining displeases the Lord. That is what God says! The journey from Egypt to Canaan, was an 11-DAY JOURNEY! These people took 40 YEARS TO GET THERE! And most of them did not get there at all.

Why? Because they had a negative mindset. They murmured and complained. They were ungrateful, fearful, whiny, and idolatrous. Because of these things, they missed out on their blessing!

When my oldest daughter was in sixth grade, I took her with me on a mission trip to Guatemala. One day, we went out shopping with some ladies from Columbia. It turned out that these ladies had a different agenda than we had; we thought we were going to do a little browsing…but they were out to boost the economy of Guatemala that day!

My daughter and I were tired, hot, thirsty, and miserable. She was fading quickly. For that matter, I was fading quickly as well! And then, my daughter started crying. "I just want to go back to the complex," she said to me. Yes—so did I! But that was not an option.

Years earlier, the Lord had spoken a phrase to me that taught me to stay focused on Him in such circumstances:

I am not the God of everything being perfect, but I am the God of victory in every circumstance and every situation.

I told my daughter, "Here is what we are going to do: We are going to talk about the things we are thankful for—but not in our whole life. Just what we are thankful for *today*. You say one, then I will say one, and let's see how high we can go."

By the time we reached Number Five, our attitudes had changed. We were seeing things from a better perspective. It wasn't long before our focus changed entirely, our spirits were lifted, and we did not feel nearly as overwhelmed.

What changed? Externally, nothing! We were still hot and thirsty. We were still tired and worn out. But we *had* changed our attitudes. And because of this—because we chose to acknowledge the good—our perception of everything around us changed. Our attitude determined our altitude, and we were flying at a much higher level by the time the shopping was finished!

Had we just stayed focused on our present situation and complained to each other, we would have only become more miserable. Complaining is a habit. Joyce Meyer says, "We can be pitiful or powerful, but we can't be both." Amen! The habit of complaining and its co-partner, self-pity, can be unlearned! There is nothing beneficial that comes from them.

Let's teach our children to acknowledge the good that is in them, in their situations, in their life. By counting our blessings and the things we appreciate, we begin to notice those more than the negative. This pleases God and promotes our faith. Remember, we don't always have the power to control our circumstances, but we do have (and can train our children to have) the power to control our response to our circumstances.

Attitude

The longer I live, the more I realize the impact of attitude on life. Attitude, to me, is more important than facts.

It is more important than past, than education, than money, than circumstances, than failures, than successes, than what other people think or say or do. It is more important than appearance, giftedness, or skill. It will make or break a company…a church…a home.[6]

~Charles Swindoll

---
[6] http://thinkexist.com/quotation/the_longer_i_live-the_more_i_realize_the_impact/296740.html

Things to realize about **ATTITUDE**:

- Attitude is something we choose
- Our attitude determines the condition of our heart
- Attitude is more important than facts
- Our attitude won't necessarily change the circumstances, but it will change us

Did you know that you *train* your children to be thankful and appreciative? If they are not trained in these things, they will not learn them!

I hate to tell you how many children I have encountered who act like the service or the blessing they receive is owed to them. Even when prompted, they eek out a little 'thank you,' but they have no idea what it means to express gratitude.

Expressing appreciation and noticing the nice things others do opens great doors of favor. Why would we want to put our children at a disadvantage when we could so easily train them to have an appreciative attitude? This is such an easy thing to train, and opens such wonderful door of favor for them.

Say to your children, "Wasn't that nice how *so-and-so* did *such-and-such* for you? They spent their own money [time, effort, etc.] to give you that gift. How does that make you feel?"

When I was little, my dad had an effective way of training us to say 'Thank you.' If he gave us something and we did not remember to say 'Thank you,' he quietly took back what he had given us. THE END! He gave not another word or thought to the incident—and trust me when I say, we quickly picked up the habit of always saying 'Thank you'!

Both of my daughters have been nannies during the summer. They've noticed that the children in their charge had not been trained to show or express appreciation. If they bought the children a fun summer gift to play with, took them out for ice cream, created an unexpected adventure for them, they'd gladly received it…but with no expression of gratitude! They both had to work all summer 'training the children to express appreciation.'

It is important for children to realize that the world does not revolve around them, and that people bless them with time, money, gifts, and so on because these people *want* to—not because they *have* to! Train your children to see it this way, and to express their gratitude. When they do this, they will stand out from the crowd, and they will open doors for more blessings to come their way! (After all, isn't it more fun to bless someone who expresses genuine appreciation instead of having an entitlement attitude?)

Throughout her time teaching, my oldest daughter has realized that appreciation is not the only thing most kids fail to learn at home—they also fail to learn many basic manners. Parents seem to think that manners will come to their children by instinct, or by magic, but manners are trained! Make sure your children learn to shake hands, to look adults in the eye, to say 'Please' and 'Thank you.' After all, not all children will end up with a teacher who decides to take their own time throughout the year to train an entire classroom in manners!

When my son was little, he often became so distracted while speaking with adults that he never looked in their eyes at all and gave them nothing but one-word responses to the questions they asked. We trained him in the importance of answering questions with full sentences (yes, even those questions where a 'Yes' would suffice!), and we told him that—after he had spoken to an adult (and answered their questions with full sentences)—he should be able to tell us what color eyes the person had.

I remember one Sunday, Mr. Click was talking to our son after church. He could hardly wait to come and report to us at a near-yell, "Mr. Click has brown eyes!"

The B.A. (**Bad Attitudes!**)…

Bad Attitudes will creep…creep…creep into our homes until they take over. You probably know without me even telling you that B.A.s are of the flesh, but you must also remember that the flesh needs discipline—and this goes for B.A.s as well! After all, at what point do you think your children will change if you do not train them to *not* embrace a B.A.? If bad attitudes, whining, temper tantrums, pouting, and begging eventually get the desired end results, do you think they will let go of these tactics? Do you think your children will suddenly start to push B.A.s away when they have found it get them extra attention? Absolutely not!

Don't make excuses for your child, or for their flesh. Don't get caught in the trap of, "She is moody," or "He is shy." Yes, each child's temperament is different. Some children are extroverted while others are introverted. And as you get to know your children through their training, you will learn what is 'personality' and what is flesh. But remember: An 'extroverted' personality is no excuse for you to allow your child to have no control over their flesh, and an 'introverted' personality is no excuse for your child to not speak to others when spoken to or to not learn to make eye contact, or dissolve when things don't go their way!

"My son is just tired." "My daughter is just excited about her birthday party." "Oh, he's just in a bad mood." Sometimes, as parents, we make excuses for our child in order to protect our own selves—in order to 'save face.' But in the long run, we are failing to train up our children to live outside of the dictates of their flesh, and the pain of this will be much greater than anything we avoid by saving face!

Our job is to train our children to manage their emotions. Their circumstances should not determine their attitude. "I'm happy because we won…" "…I'm mad because we lost" is no way for our children to live their lives! We *choose* to have joy. Our circumstances do not choose for us.

Groaning or sighing are also examples of a 'complaining mindset.'

The proper behavior is this: "That's okay, I'll obey."

Also, realize that children do not need constant attention. But those children who get constant attention come to realize they can get attention when they want.

Have you ever been to someone's house, and you could not have a conversation because their child kept interrupting? This is not 'a development stage' or 'their personality'—this is flesh!

My children used to drive me nuts when I was on the phone. This was back when phones were attached to the wall, and my children *knew*: 'Mom is tied to the phone—it's time to make dumb choices and need her help!' I had to train them in what was acceptable and what was not.

Children do not need your constant attention. And what's more, children do not need the constant attention of *anything*. Children need stimulation, but they also need to learn to be quiet. They need to learn peace.

My son did not need to take naps after the age of two and a half, but we still had him go to his room every day for an hour or an hour and a half so he could rest. Your children do not need something to always feed their eye gates and ear gates. They need time to think and enjoy peace and quiet. Quiet time is healthy every day—for children AND mom!

And remember: For all of this (the appreciation, the B.A.s, the peace and quiet), you are a model! You must model this same behavior if you want your children to follow.

We are training our children to be responsible for their choices. If they choose to listen to their flesh, our role is to correct the flesh and bring light to the difference between the spirit and the flesh. At whatever point you start this, you will begin to see the fruit.

Your children will not always have you in sight or in mind. But they *will* always have the training you gave them to make right choices!

∽ *Thoughts for Action* ∽

Key Phrases To Use With Children:

- "Disobedience requires a correction."
- "Delayed obedience is disobedience."
    - ~ You are training your child to hear and obey the voice of God on the first try; delayed obedience is the same as disobedience.
- "Obey my voice."
    - ~ You have to train your children to hear and obey your voice so they can hear and obey the voice of God.
- "I am helping you bring your flesh under control."
- "My job is to train you to have an ear to hear, so you will hear God's voice, saying, 'This is the way, walk ye in it.'"
- Always say what you do *want*, rather than what you *don't want*.
    - ~ There was a study done once with pre-school children, in which it was determined that children do not hear all the words—just the key ones. In this study, the

children were in a classroom with musical instruments on a table. The children started climbing on the table to play with the instruments. When the teacher said, "Don't get on the table," the children continued to climb on the table. All they registered was, "…on the table." Then, the teacher said, "Everyone, put your feet on the floor"—and the children responded. They did what they had heard.

~ When you tell your children what *not* to do, it is as if they are a train flying down the train tracks, and you have told them to change their direction…without giving them a different track to switch to.

~ Rather than telling your children what *not* to do, provide your children with a choice; tell your children what *to* do!

~ Some examples of this: "Walking feet" (instead of "Stop running"); "Use your inside voices"; "Listen to your spirit"; "Keep your food on your plate."

~ That gives your children clear direction—training them in the way they should go.

More Keys To Keep In Mind:

- Children are the "Master Boundary Checkers"
- Don't take disrespectful behavior personally

- We've been instructed to resist the devil, but he has turned it around for us to resist authority

- Rebellion is the opposite of submission

- Children fighting don't have to be "the norm" in your home

- Deceit has some truth in it, but it is still a lie

- Complaining is a habit. We can teach our children to acknowledge the good instead

- Attitude is everything!

- Expressing appreciation will open favorable doors for your child

- With your words, you paint a picture of who your children are. When they make a wrong choice, they are not "bad"—they simply listened to their flesh, and not to their spirit.

- As the parent, your job is to correct the flesh and help bring it under submission. You do that by dealing with the flesh—not by using our words to tear down. Use your words to build up the spirit, and to point your children in the direction you want them to go.

How to Correct

Corrections are not about you;
they are about the choice *your child made!*

The rod of correction is not the rod of anger. Remember: Corrections are not about you! They are not about 'not making Mom and Dad angry.' They are not about *pleasing you*.

With a slight adjustment in approach—changing from, 'You made a mistake because you made me angry' to 'You made a mistake because you chose to listen to your flesh'—you can experience radical change.

Your children are not *bad*—and you should never tell them they are. Your children are created in God's image. Sometimes, they simply make wrong choices.

> *Foolishness is bound up in the heart of a child, but the rod of discipline will drive it far from him.*
>
> Proverbs 22:15

> *He who spares the rod of discipline hates his son, but he who loves him disciplines diligently and punishes him early.*
>
> Proverbs 13:24

Giving the correction:

There is much controversy over the manner in which children should receive discipline. Debating those issues is not the purpose of this book. The principles in this book will work if you work them.

Whatever form of discipline is used, consistency is key. You will frustrate your child if you are inconsistent, and you will create a hardened and rebellious heart. You are actually training your child to be insensitive to God by dulling them to your words and actions.

Remember, correcting is not a power tool that is used as a threat over a child in an effort to produce acceptable behavior. This is not tyranny! Furthermore, words are not rods of correction! As soon as your conversation turns to, "If you do that one more time, you are going to…" and discipline becomes "something held over their head," the focus shifts from their ability to control their flesh and make right choice to pleasing you. Obedience is not about making you happy…you are all under God's loving command: You are supposed to do your job of training your children, and your children are supposed to do their job of learning to make right choices.

We see the rod of discipline as an external instrument—such as a wooden spoon, used to apply to the child's rear end. A hand is not right, as hands are for loving and nurturing. A belt is severe and can be dangerous.

- Give the correction in a private place.

  ~ If you are upset, send them to wait for you in your bedroom or on the stairs or in a specific chair until you can give the correction with the right attitude (don't get distracted and take too long!).

  ~ If you are sensing anger or rage, you are not in a place to correct your child. There should not be a fear of harm that your child feels, other than the pain applied to their bottom.

- If your child is small, it is good to say the same thing to them every time; there is no script—anything you say that goes along with the heart of training is awesome—but here are some suggestions:

  ~ "You have made a choice. I understand sometimes it is hard to listen to your spirit and make the right choice. Disobedience requires a correction. My job is to train you to listen to your spirit so that you will learn to listen to God's voice."

  ~ "That is why God has parents, to help you to learn to listen to your spirit. When your flesh voice gets too loud and you can't hear your spirit talking to you, Mom and Dad are here to help. Disobedience requires a correction. I am sorry you choose that, but I know next time you will listen to your spirit."

- ~ "I am not upset with you. I love you. I wish you would not have chosen this. But I understand that the flesh sometimes gets out of control, and you need help getting it back in place. That is my job. I will correct your flesh so you can make the right choices to listen to your spirit."

- Some children will go to their correction with a submitted will, and they will quickly learn to control their flesh. Other children are not quite as easy to mold to God's will! If your child tries to negotiate, tell them, "That is your flesh; if you choose to continue, that will be another correction. My job is to train you to choose to listen to your spirit so you can hear and follow God all the days of your life."

- There should be no aggression on your part—never drag, force, or threaten. This is extremely important!

- Make sure your flesh is under control before you correct them. One time, right before a correction, my son said to me, "Mom, wait! I don't think you are calm—I don't think you are listening to your spirit yet!" And he was right! I had to say, "You're right, honey. I'll wait until I calm down and can listen to my spirit. I'll be back."

- Review the infraction before giving the correction.

- Ask your child, "What does the Bible say?" If they are too young to tell you, you can tell them: "The Bible says, 'Correct your children, and they will give you rest and delight. Children, obey your parents in the Lord, for this is right.'"

- Ask your child why they are getting the correction. Their answer should be along the lines of, "Because I listened to my flesh and hit my brother over the head with my cereal bowl." Or, "Because I listened to my flesh and chose to enter into strife."

• After you review the infraction and give your child a chance to admit that they listened to their flesh, and that they understand this requires a correction, you can administer the correction. Turn them over your lap and give them three swats (or whatever you have pre-determined) on the rear. There should be no gradation of sin. "Lying gets you four swats. Hitting your brother over the head with your cereal bowl only gets you one." Flesh is flesh—and when the flesh disobeys, it requires a correction. The rod needs to be with certainty, not severity.

• When the rod is used continually, at every disobedience, it will not be associated with anger or hostility. It creates no sense of rejection. Instead—when done properly—it creates a sense of loving authority.

• Always correct the action; never correct the person. Keep it about the choice, not about the person.

- After the correction, turn your child over and set them on your lap. Love on them, hug them, and tell them you know they are growing every day to make the right choices. Then, lead them in a confession. It does not have to be the same thing every time, but it should be positive, loving, and scripture-based—something like this:

  ~ "Mom/Dad, I know you are training me to listen to my spirit and not my flesh, so that it will be well with me and I will live long on the earth. You love me, and you are training me to listen to the voice of my spirit.

- Tell your child how much you love them, and pray with them for their future.

It is okay for your child to cry, but this should not be a temper tantrum—pouting, yelling, screaming, and wailing. This is the flesh trying to rise up and manipulate you; and your job is to correct the flesh. There have been times when I had to give three corrections in a row: One for the wrong choice in the first place, and the others for the wrong attitude! You are looking for a submissive and yielded heart. If there is stubbornness, pride, or anger, you are not done with the process. You can see why it is important to be in a submitted place yourself! It is much easier to "be done with it," having gone through the motions, but not getting the compliant heart God is looking for. After all, why are we doing what we are doing? We are forming arrows that are strong, stable, and prepared to launch into the future. What you invest in this process will pay huge dividends as your children grow older. That, right there, should me motivation! Just remember, preparation time is never wasted time.

On the other hand, there might be times when the pain and disappointment your child is feeling for having made the wrong choice is discipline enough, and they will not need additional application to the flesh. Just make sure you are making this call on your own, and are not being talked out of giving the correction.

A wise son heeds and is the fruit of his father's instruction and correction, but a scoffer listens not to rebuke.
Proverbs 13:1

The correction should never be a humiliating experience—it should always be something done out of love, and your child should realize this. They should realize that you are simply helping them get their flesh under control.

As children get older and understand the concept of choosing spirit and flesh, you can ask them if they can choose for themselves or if they need help. I heard a mom say to her son as they were walking in the church parking lot, "You have until we get to the car to bring forth those peaceable fruits of righteousness by yourself and if not, and when we get to the car I will be able to help you."

One day, my son was having a tough time policing his flesh, and I asked him what he needed in order to get this under control. He said, "I think I need a correction!"

It takes time to help your child get their flesh under control. But the time you invest today will pay huge dividends down the road.

∽ Thoughts for Action ∽

Q: *Is it okay to send my child to their room, instead of correcting them?*

A: *As your child gets into their pre-teenage years, it can become a humiliating thing to them to receive a spanking—and as we have said, your child should never feel humiliated. However, I do not feel sending them to their room is especially effective. The isolation might make them feel condemned or angry. Or, they might just move on—they are out of your hair, they are now reading a book or playing with a game, but nothing in their heart is changing. Nothing in their flesh is being corrected. I found that having my children sit on the stairs—where they were still close to everyone, but were not able to 'simply move on'—was effective for us. If you do this, make sure they do not ask, "Can I get up now?" You should treat this the same way you should treat a correction—talking to them afterward about why they needed help policing their flesh, expressing love, and praying with them before they move on with their day. In this way, you can continue to train them to police their flesh on their own!*

> *The rod and reproff brings wisdom, but a child left undisciplined brings his mother to shame.*
>
> Proverbs 29:15

In the Message translations it says it this way:

> *Wise discipline imparts wisdom; spoiled adolescents embarrass their parents. Discipline your children; you'll be glad you did—they'll turn out delightful to live with.*
>
> Proverb 29: 13 & 15 Message

PUTTING IT ALL TOGETHER

Putting It All Together

*You are not perfect…
and that is all right!*

It can be difficult to remain consistent in training and disciplining your children. After all, you have more on your mind than each individual child—there are other children, cooking, jobs, and a gazillion other distractions! (Not to mention, sometimes you are tired and simply need to sit down for a minute and relax.) If your motivation in parenting is simply to end up with "good children," I can assure you that will not be motivation enough to help you be consistent, and consistent, and consistent! In this world where life is built on everything being convenient and super fast, it can be difficult to remember that parenting takes time and consistent commitment. The culture we live in does not lend itself to this kind of leadership, but this investment will pay huge dividends over time. The more consistent you are when they are young, the easier it will be when they get to those pre-teen/teenage years. At that point, the training you have done to help them make right choices and exercise internal restraint will begin to pay huge dividends.

When you realize you have made a mistake in your parenting, sit your children down and repent to them. Tell them you realize you made a mistake, and that God is holding you responsible as the steward over their lives. Tell them how you are going to do things differently—and then follow through!

As parents, we often slip into bad habits and worldly patterns. This is not worth beating ourselves up over—just realize you need to repent and change your patterns.

One time, my son came with me when I was teaching a parenting seminar out of the country. He sat on the front row, listening to my teaching on parenting, and at the end of the seminar he told me I was not doing everything right. He showed me where I had developed inconsistencies—where I was making mistakes, or was not expecting obedience on the first try. He had a list of places where I needed to improve! He was listening and giving me the Word on parenting, and he was only 12 years old!

As a parent, it is pride when we cannot say, "I made a mistake; I need to make an adjustment." Remember: We are learning as we go along. Just as we are training our children, God is training us. And it *is* a process.

You will stand accountable to God for the job you do with your children—for the diligence you take, and the effort you put in.

When you get tired or feel overwhelmed, remember that God wants to help you: ask Him to give you grace and strength, and He will!

There is definitely a process of investing as a parent. This process is sort of like compounding interest. The sooner you start the greater the dividends. Don't wait till they are "getting intimidating" before you recognize how important consistent and steady training is to having the kind of family you dreamed of.

The world is looking for hope for the family. 1 Timothy 4:12 says, "Let no one look down on your youth, but be an example (pattern) for the believers in speech, in conduct, in love, in faith, and in purity."

When God designed the family He had an idea of how it would succeed. As you purpose to follow His simple advice, I believe you will get the results your hearts long for. No, life isn't going to be perfect. In fact, it's going to be messy. What better way to prepare than having a family who is purposing to walk after the spirit and not after the flesh. After all, when our families are listening to their spirit they will have parents who are purposing to make right choices, raising Children Who Make Right Choices.

∾ *Final Thoughts for Action* ∾

If you are experiencing a lack of success...

- Check your consistency.

- Are you definite in your convictions? Are you intimidated?

- Don't look at what you are going through—look at where you are going.

- Do not get discouraged.

- Are your children getting enough attention *without* disobeying?

- Remember: Your purpose is higher than just raising 'good kids.'

- When your children are spirit-controlled and spirit-led, they will be a delight!

- Your children should be able to discern the difference between spirit and flesh, and should be able to choose (correctly!) between the two.

- They should be able to choose their attitude and submit to authority.

- The benefits of children who are marked for God:

    ~ They will have inner security.

    ~ Their personality will shine.

    ~ They will live above their circumstances.

    ~ They will be free from the dictates of the flesh!

Lean on, trust in, and be confident in the Lord with all your heart and mind and do not rely on your own insight or understanding. In all your ways know, recognize, and acknowledge Him, and He will direct and make straight and plain your paths.

Proverbs 3:5-6

Other Training Aids from Diane Tohline

Speak the Word of God over your children to frame their future.

I compiled this stack of scriptures when my children were young so I could speak the Word of God over them.

There are 80 Scriptures printed on plastic coated cards. The size makes them easy to put in your purse, or you can take them off the ring to place them on your mirror or refrigerator.

Scripture cards: $7.00

Parenting with God as your GPS

Parenting with God as your GPS helps us see where we are going. It maps our course to help us stay on track. This 5 CD teaching series covers:

- What is God's purpose for us as parents? What does he see as our role?

- How do we train our children to listen to their spirit and make wise choices?

5 CD teaching series $20.00

- What is God's purpose in training our children?
- How do we train our children to hear and obey God's voice?
- What does God say about discipline?

For ordering information, go to
http://DianeTohline.com/category/store
Diane can be contacted through her website:
http://DianeTohline.com